Border-Listening/Escucha-Liminal

Volume 2, 2021

Alexandre Herbetta
Ana Ruiz Valencia
D'Andrade
Daniela Avellar
Fabián Ávila Elizalde
Paulo Antonio Kalankó
Reiko Yamada
Rui Chaves
Nora Castrejón
Teresa Díaz de Cossio
Vered Engelhard

Edited by
Alejandra Luciana Cárdenas

Radical Sounds Latin Americc

PUBLISHED BY *CONTINGENT SOUNDS PRESS*
within the framework of
RADICAL SOUNDS LATIN AMERICA 2021
www.radicalsoundslatinamerica.com

ISBN 978-3-00-070411-6
Anton-Saefkow-Platz 13
10369 Berlin, DE

Graphic design by Alejandra Luciana Cárdenas.
Printed in Germany by Online-Druck GmbH & Co. KG.
All rights reserved.

This book was published for the third edition of the festival Radical Sounds Latin America, a festival exploring cutting-edge Latin American music, co-curated by Alejandra Luciana Cardenas and Talia Vega.

Radical Sounds Latin America was made possible thanks to the support of Musicboard Berlin and the kind collaboration of Silent Green, Cashmere Radio, KM28, Nuts and Bolts, Roots Radicals and HÖR.

Supported by Musicboard Berlin GmbH

Contents

Introduction
Alejandra Luciana Cárdenas 5

An Amplified Echo, a Carbonated Resonance
Daniela Avellar 11

Sonic Cartography in the Rímac Watershed: On the Contemporaneity of a Pre-Columbian Acoustic Ecology
Vered Engelhard 31

Resounding Epistemologies of Conflict: Auralities in Colombia's Historical Memory
Ana Ruiz Valencia 59

¿Un arte sonoro menor?: *Dosis de escucha* (2018) y *El aula de los ruidos* (2019)
Nora Castrejón/Fabián Avila Elizalde 91

Indigenous and Anticapitalist Sounds: Musical Practices to Pollinate the Brazilian Caatinga
Alexandre Herbetta/Paulo Antonio Kalankó 121

32 instrucciones para escuchar con/en una epidemia global
Rui Chaves 147

Listening for Alida Vázquez: A Life in Electronic Music between Migration, Race and Gender
Teresa Díaz de Cossio 161

On Temperament and Tempering
Reiko Yamada 179

Noise Vivarium: Spectral Radicalism
D'Andrade 203

Introduction

The first volume of this publication (2020) made the creation of a second volume urgent (as the second has recently paved the way for a third), because it proposes a challenge that does not exhaust itself but that constantly raises new questions. Furthermore, in the past two years, during which the first two volumes were conceived, the catastrophe of the COVID-19 pandemic hit us with waves of lockdowns, curfews and endless obituaries. Changes of colossal proportions lashed out (with different intensities) around the globe, and marked the uncertain landscape we now find ourselves in. What's more, if a global pandemic of this magnitude wasn't sufficient, this crisis has become a sort of prequel in the media and in political discourse, setting the tone for the upcoming Crisis. The Crisis with a capital C created by Man with a capital M: the crisis of ecological destruction that is *yet to come.* Yet, this double rupture forms the fissures from which Border-Listening/Escucha-Liminal pours out.

As a new awareness of catastrophe grows in the West, in the global South, some have been building lives around ecological devastation for generations. Long before environmentalists introduced the term "climate change" to the vocabulary of the twentieth century—an achievement of planetary-scale computation and scientific prediction—*others* had no need of these mathematical calculations to notice the devastating Man-made environmental degradation of their lands, rivers and oceans. Scenarios of deforestation,[1] desertification, the disappearance of lagoons[2] or valleys are common currency in the southern reaches of the world, where the extractivist model that was once a colonial system is now promoted by neo-extractivist governments. Hence, for those who have already lived amid ecological devastation, the announcements of new times of crisis can bring about as much estrangement as familiarity.

---

1 In this regard, the news about deforestation in the Amazon rainforest tend to tackle the last fifty years, during which these activities have intensified and become industrialized, but the dramatic transformation of land into plantations, resulting in soil degradation and deforestation dates back to the sixteenth century (brazilwood extraction), and can equally be seen in the eighteenth century (the sugarcane cycle) and in the rubber boom of both the eighteenth and twentieth centuries.

2 For example, the impact of mining in the Cajamarca Region, Peru, where the mining project Minera Yanacocha (producer and exporter of gold and silver) irreversibly destroyed the main supplies of water safe for human consumption in the region, leaving large holes in the land where previously there were agricultural activities, lagoons, and rivers. This project caused the disappearance of many lagoons, the principal among these bears the name of the mining site, Yanacocha (an aquifer formation with a surface area of 3.5 hectares). See: Wiener Fresco, Raúl and Juan Torres Polo. (2014). *La Gran Minería: ¿paga los impuestos que debería pagar? El caso Yanacocha.* Lima: Latindadd.

Our struggles, joys and contradictions closely resemble the vibrations of our territories—mountainous, seismic, volcanic, arid, fertile. Thus, this editorial endeavor takes listening as a point of departure from which to explore these geographies, their local historical conditions, asymmetries, and the practices that remain unheard. In this sense, this project aspires to be a liminal site, a subversion, a space to experiment, a question mark.

We believe that this strategy has the potential to inject unpredictability and contingency into the monolithic Euro-Western narratives. Thus, if we sneak a grain of sand from the peripheral positions of the global South (and its diasporas) into the fashionable and growing sound disciplines, it means that this edition has been fruitful. Ultimately, our main intention is to serve as a decentering force within contemporary listening practices and debates surrounding sound.

With that purpose in mind, we invited the collaborators of this volume (Ana Ruiz Valencia, Daniela Avellar, Fabián Avila and Nora Castrejón, D'Andrade, Paulo Antonio Kalankó and Alexandre Herbetta, Reiko Yamada, Rui Chaves, Teresa Díaz de Cossío and Vered Engelhard) to articulate and explore alternative practices of listening that fall outside the bounds of cripplingly heteronormative

hegemonic structures, while also engaging with
the ethical dilemmas of our age. We encourage
and welcome essays and artistic research about
soundscapes and sonic stories from Latin American,
but also multispecies, intersectional approaches,
indigenous ontologies and positions that contend
with the Western vocabulary.

I would like to especially thank the careful attention
of our proofreaders (Kirstin Cameron for the English
texts and Paloma Reaño for the Spanish texts) and
the authors of the essays that make up this publication for their patience and support throughout the
editorial process of this issue.

Alejandra Luciana Cárdenas

ALEJANDRA LUCIANA CÁRDENAS

An Amplified Echo, a Carbonated Resonance

DANIELA AVELLAR is a researcher, writer and DJ based in Rio de Janeiro, Brazil. She graduated in Psychology before gaining a master's degree in Contemporary Studies of the Arts at the Universidade Federal Fluminense. Currently, a member of the doctorate program in Media and Culture Studies at Universidade Federal do Rio de Janeiro. Ms. Avellar frequently writes for academic and independent publications, as well as for exhibitions, and is co-curator of the independent space *Refresco*, of an artistic residency program in Rio de Janeiro's port area, and the Latin American sound art exhibition *Somarumor* (2019).

Multispecies soundscape and affective echo

> Our tools of analysis block our ability to see our objects.
> —Anna Tsing, *Viver nas ruínas: paisagens multiespécies no antropoceno*

> Material responds to material, not just to us.
> —Anna Tsing, *Viver nas ruínas: paisagens multiespécies no antropoceno*

It is always good to open a text with an insoluble dilemma, or with a mystery. With the words presented here, I try to dance, or to sing a song—at least to align my movements with my objects of choice, produce entanglements and begin to search together (2. Ibid., 38). Of course, to be fair to those reading this paper, I should explain what this is about... so... let me try:

I believe that where there is air, there is sound. I also believe that there is always something else sounding while we hear. If we focus on one sound (try this now), there is something more there that affects our listening. Sound is always layered, in sounds over sounds. In these lines, I will try to tell you a story conducted by listening, and also conducted, as John Cage desired,[1] by the songs we miss, inspired

---
[1] John Cage was a famed mushroom enthusiast. He used to forage for them, and composed sound pieces for, and based on, what he

by the noises we cannot hear, the sounds that we have never had the chance to listen to (due to the limitations of our human interface), which is why we miss them. Just like Cage's beloved spores and their sibilant music (3. Ibid., 49). Here we face hearing as a tool that can be used to perceive things. Through sound, we can recognize the difference between hot and cold, or the intensity of a rainy day. Nature is always singing; every animal is a sound maker, including me, and probably you. A few days ago, I heard this discussed on the Future Ecologies podcast *The nature of sound* (2019). It is important to note that some of this paper's references come from podcasts; to write about sound is to be open to what can be transmitted orally.

To explore this more deeply, the question is not just about the position of hearing and aurality in comparison with the visual domain and the eye. As Suely Rolnik puts it, we could think about communication as not being the sole way to guide our existence (2018, 52). In this light, sound is a route to understanding the world and capturing its signals, thinking about the effects of sound on our body that go beyond cognitive attributes. That is to say, sound is always relational; it connects with the series of encounters that constitute being alive; encounters "between people, things, landscapes, ideas, works

---

observed in the spores he found.

of art, political situations and others etc." (ibid., 53). These kinds of friction produce changes in our diagrams of forces, producing different effects that open up new ways to feel, to see and to hear. These encounters affect us. Relations are mediated by language, but what I am seeking to achieve here is a text that rejects logocentrism and wants to traverse affect, intuition, thinking about subjects beyond the individual, and listening beyond its physiological aspects (or cochlear patterns, as in the important work of Seth Kim-Cohen [2009[2]]).

To listen is to be at the encounter with an *other,* an *other* that is always difference. This is my reason for starting with a profound dilemma—because the other, or the object, does not exist outside ourselves, but within. When we talk about communication and cognition, it is true that we seek a common language, something familiar. Suely Rolnik tells us, however, that we might think of an experience outside the subject and its supposed interiority, yet the "other" effectively lives within us by the way of affects (2. Ibid., 111). This experience is part of an intensive resonance (a term we will explore later in more depth). As Anna Tsing points out, referring to bacteria as the "other" (the example may seem random, but is not

---

[2] It is important to note that when Seth Kim-Cohen discusses what he terms "non-cochlear", he emphasizes listening as an experience mediated by language. However, as I do, Kim-Cohen practices elliptical displacements, rejecting hermetic positions.

random at all, as you will see...), 90% of our cells are bacteria; they are with us and we need them—our bodies become with them, we are because of them. Moreover, this changes how we think about human action in the world: how can we act as we do if we do not include the other species that make us? (Tsing 2019, 73).

I said I came here to tell you a story. A story is always fictitious. I like to think with Ursula K. Le Guin (1986), that storytelling can be a way to tell about and collect the stuff of living. Fiction can be less about the triumph of a hero, or the story of a hunter and their prey. Le Guin tells us that before the weapon, before a gun, there was a bag, a container, a net, a sack to reunite questions (Haraway 2016, 40). I discovered Le Guin's stories through reading Donna Haraway's work. I use her words here to try to describe the movement I am scoring here: in these lines, I seek to make in a sympoietic way, as:

> sympoiesis is a simple word; it means 'making-with'. Nothing makes itself; nothing is really autopoietic or self-organizing. In the words of the Inupiat computer "world game", earthlings are never alone. That is the radical implication of sympoiesis. Sympoiesis is a word proper to complex, dynamic, responsive, situated, historical systems. It is a word for worlding-with, in company. (Haraway 2016, 58)

Fermentation is a collaborative practice that positions us in a process of cooperation with more than human beings. In it, we are co-participants in a movement of microbiological transformation that is markedly interspecies. As Anna Tsing indicates, these transformations are what is important for life on earth—located at a distance from the arborescent decisions of independent and private subjects (relating to Rolnik's ideas), they consist of stories that develop through contamination, transforming encounters into events (Tsing 2015, 29). Every gathering in this case is therefore bigger than the sum of two parts. Fermentation is also an activity capable of preserving (while simultaneously transforming) food, contributing to a less pasteurized and homogeneous consumption. I like to think, with Lauren Fournier, that fermentation is an exercise of futurity (Fournier 2020, 100)—another term to which we will return later (I am just filling my bag with terms and ideas).

The story continues, telling you that I have been practicing fermentation with an old friend and have discovered new ways to eat, cook, follow a recipe, pass the time, smell and listen. We often film ourselves with our hands in action and alongside the juicy images, we also perceive the sounds that are typical of the actions of bubbles formed by the encounter between "good" bacteria and the right measure of sugar or salt (the ingredients that scare the dominance of "evil" colonies). The carbon dioxide in question produces sound reverberations that sometimes border on the inaudible, just as the existence of microorganisms belongs to the order of the invisible.

On one specific day (although maybe my friend does not even remember, and this is simply the obsessive fetish of sound researchers), we perceived a sound that could only be heard by the cellphone's recorder, and was not directly audible to our human ears alone. We listened to this sound only later, just after it had been captured. This situation had me thinking for days, about questions such as: what are the vibration noises of fermentation? How does this sound articulate its power to disrupt our colonial and normative ways of eating, as well as how we perceive the world and relate to each other? Does sound research create evidence or build an empirical world from listening? It is true that soundscapes are always leaving their places of origin behind, transforming an object into an event. In the same way, I believe that fermentation transforms food, prolonging it into a future (another temporal conception), while also, as said before, preserving it. Both cases are an extension of singularities in difference, like a carbonated echo where the signal drags or spreads... What is that sound? Does it also have the power to dismantle our more stratified ways and ideas? What kind of listening is involved in this scenario, or performative gesture?

One way to enter this kind of movement, even knowing the difficulties, and therefore   always trying not to capture the material through a solely (or too) human comprehension (Tsing 2019, 144), is to follow Bernie Krause's ideas about biophony. Krause was one of the invited researchers who spoke with Future Ecologies:

> When I was writing these books and trying to describe what I was hearing, what I found was— is there's a tremendous paucity of language to describe what we hear because we're a visual culture. So there's a lot of material describing the visual, but almost none— just aren't very many words to describe what we hear. So I took the idea of Murray Schafer's soundscape, which is all the sound that reaches our ear, and in working with kids, I had to ask them when they went outside listen to sound, what were the sources of those different sounds? Are they mechanical sources? Are they human sources? Are they natural sources? What are the ways in which those sounds appear to you? How do you describe them? And so at one point in the late 90s, I introduced the term biophony, meaning the natural sounds that we hear, the collective sound that we hear from a particular habitat, but it's just the natural sounds. It's not anything else. It's all the bird sounds and insects, mammals, amphibians, and so on. (Krause 2019)

About landscapes, Anna Tsing says that we often "use this term to imagine a backdrop for human action." However, if we worry about habitability, we will have to figure out how to make landscapes animated, and the protagonists of our stories. Tsing says that "we need landscapes, spatialized enactments of livability" and that her landscapes "are a multispecies moots, enactments of the possibilities of living together" (Tsing 2019, 94). Can we think about a multispecies soundscape? Of course we could! We must. If Tsing reacts to an idea of landscape that slips between the unpredictable and the gathering of organisms, how can we fail to consider an idea of landscape that is not attached to the question of the visual? Between Krause's biophony and the notion of polyphony, Anna Tsing creates a good score:

> Polyphony is music in which autonomous melodies intertwine. In Western music, the madrigal and the fugue are examples of polyphony. These forms seem archaic and strange to many modern listeners because they were superseded by music in which a unified rhythm and melody holds the composition together. In classical music that replaced baroque, unity was the goal; this was 'progress' in exactly the sense I have been discussing: a unified coordination of time. In 20th century rock and roll, this unity takes the form of a strong beat, hinting at the listener's heart. We are used to listening to music with a single perspective. When I learned polyphony, it was a revelation (...). I was forced to pick out separate, simultaneous melodies and to listen for the moments of

> harmony and dissonance they created together. This kind of noticing is just what is needed to appreciate the multiple temporal rhythms and trajectories of the assemblage. (Tsing 2019, 152)

A dance floor is certainly a good place for encounters. However, let us forget the four-beat rhythm for a while, and allow space for a concert of experimental noise: this situation is a better scene against which to think about the kind of encounter and effect described above. Alternatively, we could simply think about a group of people engaged together in the fermenting process. When we are at my friend's kitchen fermenting food, it is difficult to choose a soundtrack. We usually handle our invisible companies with just a little conversation, talking about the week's events and light topics, in gentle voices. If we follow John Cage's example and equalize both sound and music, we could say that conversation is a way to compose a sound piece. We also know that, when fermenting food, from the perspective of the sonic event, one should expect that inaudible or low frequency sounds are part of the polyphony that is present—a multispecies soundscape that involves different forms of life being together, perceiving each other (ibid., 66).

As we finish our fermentation activities, I ask myself what I have heard. It is never a simple question. And there is no right answer. To pose this question to myself is to reconstitute it, repeatedly. There is no representational paradigm for the signals. The object always returns (the dilemma). It is like the listening protocols sessions from artistic collective Ultra-Red[3], whose works are more about hearing-compositions than sound-compositions. The activist group began investigating and creating in the 1990s, in parallel with the HIV-acceptance movement and its struggle against homophobia and other social oppressions. Tato Taborda, referring to David Lapoujade's ideas, talks about the use of the term "sympathy" to account for "a movement in which observer and object coincide and vibrate in synchronism in the incandescent core of the meaning of the observed object, a core inaccessible by any other method of approximation" (2021, 93). There is a certain vibration within the core of the object, a dissonance; that is why the beat is not a good metaphor here. There is an inaudible vibration inside the Kimchi container, or the Kombucha jar. The object then reveals itself as an object-subject (...) endowed with a pathos with which, in a flashing instant unlike any score, the observer's pathos coincides and merges, vibrating with it instantly and violently commotion. In the glow of the privileged instant in which

---

3 For further detail regarding UltraRed, listen to the Serpentine's Gallery podcast episode *On Practice: Listening.* Available at: https://open.spotify.com/episode/1cWsAIzKDjihuCXSXjsLsl?si=ZxdjLy43Qtumx7u7tI0I_g&dl_branch=1

intuition occurs" (ibid., 93), we "sympathize" with matter insofar as we apprehend it as pure movement (Lapoujade 2017, 62).

Recipes are open scores

> Today, our topping is carp, made into small brown nuggets (...). It is tantalisingly rich and spicy, and I ask how it is made. FamTsoi explains, "You have a fish. You add salt". She falters; that is it. I imagine myself in the kitchen with a raw salty fish dripping in my hand. Language has met its limit. The trick of cooking is in the bodily performance, which is not easy to explain. The same is true for mushroom picking, more dance than classification. It is a dance that partners here with many dancing lives.
> —Anna Tsing, *Viver nas ruínas: paisagens multiespécies no antropoceno*

And I remember a teacher who taught raw food classes, at the university, with a very political perspective. She said, "oh, do you want me to give you a recipe? The recipe is: take the banana, peel the banana. That's it." I also remember my mother when I tried to ferment yogurt at home for the first time. (In this case it is not about the relation to the recipe.) I tried to follow the recipe like an hermetic score. I had almost forgotten that my mother, like my grandmother, had fermented things throughout my life, using only their intuition as a guide. Fermentation seems to lead us to handle recipes like open scores. Their notation is something less representational and more connected to a direction to action. If it says to you, "act," then let us peel the banana.

Until now, we have looked at ways to encounter and handle objects that can be channeled through sympathy. Remember what I said about resonance? If we open the score, we can ask ourselves if the principle that guides the kind of relation we are discussing here is not the echo, but the resonances of sympathy (or even sympoietic resonances, why not?) vibrations. If resonance, as Tato Taborda puts it, is spontaneous and caused by frequency affinities (acoustic, or affective and subjective, to return to Suely Rolnik), it refers to a mutual cycle. Resonance encompasses an encounter between two bodies that is more than the sum of the parts (Taborda 2021, 19). It is also a mode of relation that activates ways of being and individual and collective vibrations that connects us to the forces of life, helping us to do worldings (ibid., 21). Between us and the food we ferment, there is more mode of relation than merely two agents facing each other—we make ourselves vibrate. The cabbage, salt, and bacteria all have their own voices and scores, but these scores inhabit us, somehow, latently.

If we think about resonance between two humans, we could think about different languages and gestures that create vibration from two voices, creating space. This is unlike the echo, when an input implies "a wave that propagates until rest." An echo only repeats the original message (2. Ibid., 119). Bodies, whether human or more than human, when in resonance, produce modulation since participating in a different process of sound propagation occurs when we allow ourselves to be grasped by identifiable frequencies. Taborda says that in the case of an echo, bodies act like conductive vehicles that move the fragments but without making displacements, resulting in a passive relation (ibid., 125).

Meanwhile, Brandon LaBelle reminds us that the dub mix of reggae has delays and echoes as central aspects. This sonic structure presents rhythms and tonalities that make us think about itinerant lives and migration, like forces of resistance in a sense that dislocates, through remixes, origins "in favor of flexibility and transience, resilience and displacement" (LaBelle 2018, 117).

> From within the electronic delays saturating the music, one may detect the ecstatic arrival of a type of unification; according to a logic of displacement, of singularity always being prolonged into repetitions, of not quite the same - delays are not duplications,

> rather they spiral in and around origin, mutating as they go; from within this echo world (...) reggae culture constructs a form of wholeness. (ibid., 117)

When thinking about the migration of sound, practices of diversality, diffraction, and echo form, in the face of the logics of western colonial capitalism, as LaBelle suggests, "a type of archipelagic imaginary by which to skirt the grip of the colonial hand" (ibid., 118). We can transform our soundscape-metaphor again. Since we can now think not only about the Jamaican soundsystem, but can also look to the practice of sampling, we must begin to think about rap and hip-hop songs, in which language seems less immutable as violent forces consolidate it. In this kind of music, there is a flow, an energy that reverberates in something that vibrates through repetition.

Thing of the past, signal of the future

> The fleeting and punctuated event of sound is one of transience and transition; an itinerant and migratory sensorial matter, sound is both a thing of the past and a signal of the future; it point us toward what has happened - for every sound is an index of an event that, by the time we hear it, has already transpired - while equally pulling us forward by echoing beyond, toward a distance over there. The articulated presence of any sound, at one and the same moment, is to be found in its disappearance and its becoming.
> — Brandon LaBelle, *Sonic Agency: Sound and emergent Forms of Resistance*

26 Here I feel kinship with the artist, and my friend, Jonas Van, who talks on the FERA LIVRE (2021) podcast (in the episode *Epistemologia do gesto* [Epistemology of gesture]) about a refusal in relation to the separation between bodies and matter. He seeks an ecology (for lack of a better term) that does not measure up to an ecology centered on the white, male and cisgender subject. This kind of practice denies forms of life, worldings, and imposes on us a certain way of dealing with time. Fermentation places us in another relation with temporality; it is a way to reconnect with practices that have been silent and make them louder. It is a way of reclaiming. I often talk with Jonas about fermentation. On this podcast, he says that fermentation is something that happens

all the time, because we are transmuting matter and energy all the time. And this time doesn't fit the linear, chronological model. Things do not necessarily have an end, but we must die somehow, to live. When you presuppose rottenness, things recreate life. It is like that with fermentation, sometimes. We make a lot of Kimchi out of cabbage—also as an exercise in futurity. Yesterday, Jonas Van wrote to me about a dream he had; we were together inside something similar to a time machine. There are vibrations in his dream that inhabit me in latency.

Yes, our ability to hear objects must still face a thick and misty cloud, created in part by the difficulties of our methodological apparatus. Nevertheless, it is no use not to try, or to insist on a hermetic and mute relationship. I cannot just read things and tell you aseptically what I have learned. I tell stories as I try to write, to talk, or to sound like someone who is excited about something new and about a new life appearing. It is a vibrant matter[4]—the world, my bag, these lines are full of such matter. Like the Kombucha that grows in my kitchen now. Maybe like me, you, my computer, a cat that stares at me. Scores for us all to become with.

---
[4] In a sense that Jane Bennett (2010) tells us about.

References

Bennett, Jane. 2010. *Vibrant Matter: A political ecology of things*. USA: Duke University Press.

Fournier, Lauren. 2020. "Fermenting Feminism as Methodology and Metaphor: Approaching Transnational Feminist Practices through Microbial Transformation." *Environmental Humanities* (May).

Haraway, Donna. 2015. *Staying With the Trouble: Making Kin in the Chthulucene*. USA: Duke University Press.

Kim-Cohen, Seth. 2009. *In the Blink of an Ear: Toward a Non-cochlear Sonic Art*. New York: Continuum.

LaBelle, Brandon. 2018. Sonic Agency: Sound and emergent Forms of Resistance. London: Goldsmiths Press.

Lapoujade, David. 2017. *As potências do tempo*. São Paulo: N-1 edições.

Le Guin, Ursula K. 1986. "The Carrier Bag Theory of Fiction" Last modified June 30, 2021. https://otherfutures.nl/uploads/documents/le-guin-the-carrier-bag-theory-of-fiction.pdf

Rolnik, Suely. 2018. *Esferas da Insurreição: Notas para uma vida não cafetinada*. São Paulo: N-1 Edições.

Taborda, Tato. 2021. *Resonâncias: vibrações por simpatia e frequências de insurgência*. Rio de Janeiro: Editora da Universidade Federal do Rio de Janeiro.

Tsing, Anna. 2015. *The Mushroom at the End of the World*. New Jersey: Princeton University Press.

Tsing, Anna. 2019. *Viver nas ruínas: paisagens multiespécies no antropoceno*. Brasília: IEB – Mil Folhas.

Ana Raylander, Diran Castro, Jonas Van. "EP: Epistemologia do gesto", 24 February, 2021, on FERA LIVRE.

Future Ecologies, 2019. "FE2.5 - The Nature of Sound" Last modified June 30, 2021. https://www.futureecologies.net/listen/fe-2-5-the-nature-of-sound

On Practice: Listening. Serpentine Podcast. 5 March, 2021. https://open.spotify.com/episode/1cWsAIzKDjihuCXSXjsLsl?si=7wGEnUF1S9-faeINyTZhow&dl_branch=1

Sonic Cartography in the Rímac Watershed: On the Contemporaneity of a Pre-Columbian Acoustic Ecology

VERED ENGELHARD is a Peruvian artist and scholar based in New York. Their research centers on acoustic ecologies and Pre-Columbian imaginaries, instruments and infrastructures. Utilizing portable instruments like flutes, *pututos*, shakers, chimes and recorders, and amplifying present elements such as wind, water and stones; their music is always emergent of the place of its happening. Engelhard works with the Asociación de Siembra y Cosecha de Agua, a collective dedicated to research and activism in watersheds on the southern Pacific coast, and is a member of the OPERA Ensemble, a group of composers and performers working in the intersections of music and environmentalism. Engelhard is a PhD candidate in Latin American cultural studies in Columbia University.

Overview   (Underhearing)

The following article considers a series of intersections between the practice of sonic cartography, environmental activism, and academic research. It functions as the baselines of sonic maps that are yet to be made, articulating the historical and practical grounds, methodological concerns, material limitations, and ethical commitments involved in cartographic practice. In conjunction with this articulation, the article poses several questions: What can territorial approaches to mapping add to the hegemonic modes of representation in planning? How can putting listening at the center of mapmaking intervene in the colonially-inherited, vision-oriented tradition of cartography? In what ways can the collective practice of mapping, when approached from the standpoint of motion, transform our communal relations and sense of place?

More than making a map, the primary concern is to approach listening-based practices of community mapping in Huarochirí within the context of work carried out as part of the Asociación de Siembra y Cosecha de Agua (ASyCA), dedicated primarily to the implementation of the hydrological system known in the Andes as water sowing and harvesting (*siembra y cosecha de agua*). Both an ancestral and cosmopolitan knowledge, the process of water sowing involves capturing, deriving, retaining, and filtering water in the headwaters (*cabeceras de cuenca*) of the mountain peaks (*punas*). Rainwater crowns and then enters the mountain—subsoils are nurtured, biodiversity proliferates—and is made available year-round to be harvested during the dry season, by directing it to neighboring settlements and cultivation areas. This system has the potential to secure food sovereignty and control over natural resources, thus strengthening the networks between neighboring communities by means of sharing the watershed. This ancestral technology also operates as a living archive, in the sense that it revalorizes the histories of these communities by recalling practices and modes of living that lie forgotten under the current precarious infrastructures of dependence to, in this case, the metropolis of the Peruvian capital, Lima.

Huarochirí is a province located in the Andes at the headwater of the Rímac River, the main water source for the city of Lima. Thus, from the standpoint of water, Lima depends more on Huarochirí than the reverse. In the context of our climate crisis, and the specific challenges posed by this particular ecosystem (characterized by cycles of flood and drought), listening to and walking the ways of the water is a vital strategy for a deep engagement with the territory through an opening up, in the words of Anna

Tsing, of "the curiosity that seems to me the first requirement of collaborative survival in precarious times" (Tsing, 2015,19).

The territory, in terms of the practice of water sowing and harvesting, is understood as the different interconnected ecosystems in the same basin or sub-basin, with its present, past, and potential headwaters (Mora, 2020). A trained eye can identify the traces of infrastructure where water used to be harvested. These traces of hydric infrastructure are also traces of ancestral practices for the use and maintenance of water. The identification of these traces points to an abundance that lies latent in the mountains, but has been unknown to the communities in their lifetimes. Gregorio Ríos, technical promoter, a senior master builder from San Pedro de Casta in Huarochirí, and the president of ASyCA, states that water sowing is a "forgotten" practice. From this statement we understand that the implementation of the system is a work of remembering. Ríos speaks of the work of the Asociación as "the implementation of a new structure, following the traces of the ancient ones (*siguiendo las huellas de los antiguos*)."[1] These traces are imprinted in the mountain—they are depressions in the soil that can hold and channel running water, the vestiges of pre-Columbian[2] stone

---

[1] Asociación de Siembra y Cosecha de Agua -ASyCA meeting on April 17th 2021, San Pedro de Casta.

[2] I name Columbus as a reference point rather than 'the Hispanic' in order to affirm a more continental idea of colonialism, in line with Sylvia Wynter's essay *1492: A New World View*.

infrastructure for retention and capture, as well as underground conduits and filtering caves. Water sowing and harvesting are taught and learned by walking with and listening to the paths of the water, from the moment it arrives from the clouds. The practice responds, both historically and cyclically, to an integrated sense of territory, and to the shared necessities of its communities.

In response to the systematization of the science of cartography, various practices of community mapping (*mapeo comunitario*) have emerged that point towards other forms of representation of histories and life cycles grounded on the sensorial (Sletto, Bryan, et al., 2013). Representation here works towards an understanding that the shared necessities of communities are entangled with poetics and idiosyncrasies, with fantastic senses of the future and with histories that lie dormant. In working with ASyCA, mapping thus weaves itself into the process of remembering, that is, the implementation of the hydrological system, communicating other forms of habitation and honoring a heritage that is imprinted in the mountain, but which hegemonic systems of historical recording invalidate as fiction rather than fact (De la Cadena, 2015)[3].

---

[3] Marisol De la Cadena speaks of how "a central technology of history" is "evidence, or the reasonable composition of facts as signs of events." She makes the case for ahistorical beings, which cannot be proven and are therefore relegated to the realm of the non-existent. De la Cadena, Marisol. 2015. *Earth Beings: Ecologies of Practice Across Andean Worlds* , 147. Durham: Duke University Press.

Extractivist City
(hegemonic systems of historical recording)

I chose to begin this piece of writing in the city of Lima as a gesture of positioning, since it is where I come from and where I began to walk and listen, and make the point that the foundation of the city of Lima marks a tradition of shaping the territory in alienation from the land (*tierra*)[4]. It is this tradition that the previously-mentioned hegemonic systems of historical recording inaugurate, dehistoricize, and perpetuate. Lima's inception as the "City of Kings" in the sixteenth century brought with it the imposition of a sedentary society of settlers that established the city as the centralizing point of accumulation of the Viceroyalty of Peru and the principal communication channel between the New World and the Spanish Empire. The aim of establishing the port city was to effect a shift in the center of imperial power away from the pre-existing Incan empire, with its political center in Cusco, in the heart of the Andes. Having Cusco, nicknamed "the belly of the world," as an administrative imperial center, corresponds to an understanding of the territory as an interconnected landmass, and of the practices of circulation of resources as processes integral to the territory's

---

[4] For more on this see also: del Castillo, Juan Manuel. "Lima la fértil: De la inconsistencia del discurso de la ciudad-desierto" *Archdaily, August 5, 2016.*

geography (Kaulicke, 2008). The port city reflects a different set of circulation priorities, in which the center of accumulation sits beside the boats that will take the resources to an alien land far away. The re-centralization of power established a form of accumulation in which lifeforms, otherwise conceived as beings that come from the landmass and are destined to go back into it, are deterritorialized as alienated resources that ought to be taken away, by sea, to another—invisible yet subordinating—place. From its inception, the planning of this city presupposes an erasure of the places, beings, and resources that build and sustain its territory.

From the standpoint of the ecosystem, this geographic expansion of life came at the expense of many of the life cycles already in place (and consequently at the expense of lives themselves). Thus, from an ecological standpoint, the so-called conquest can be understood as an expansion of the existing ecology that necessarily brought with it the introduction of new cycles sustained by the brutal eradication of others.

The first official map of Lima dates back to the seventeenth century, and is emblematic of the slow violence (Nixon, 2011) of physical and mnemonic obliteration of the existing ecosystem by Spanish colonialism. Drawn from the perspective of someone reaching the city from the ocean, the author specifically arrives at the port of Callao, the largest port on the Pacific coast at the time, and still the largest in the country today. The land is represented as a void—only the Rímac River, the gridded plan of Lima (at the time a walled city), and the mountain behind it (now part of the city), crowned with a cross,[5] are shown. Cultivation, irrigation systems, *puquiales*[6], *humedales*[7], settlements, the *qhapac ñan*[8], the *lomas*[9], and most living beings are all rendered non-existent. Also non-existent are newly developed practices such as the importation of cattle, and the overuse of water from the Rímac required to feed them, uncontrolled deforestation for building with wood and fabricating vegetable carbon (practices the locals did not engage in), all of which contributed to an "ecological rupture" (Rostworowski 1981, 35) that materialized as the overall drying out of the

---

5 The mountain was renamed San Cristobal, although it is also considered a *tirakuna*, a living entity dotted with, for lack of a better word, spirit. For more on this see: Marisol De la Cadena, *Earth Beings*, 100-112.

6 "Outcrops of infiltrated water, emerging from underground". *Cartilla 2*. Asociación de Siembra y Cosecha de Agua -ASyCA, forthcoming.

7 A group of *puquiales*. ASyCA, 2021.

8 Incan road system.

9 An ecosystem particular to the Pacific-facing central and northern coastal territory, where green areas form on particular heights as a result of contact with moist clouds and the mountain.

Figure 1. The oldest map of Lima, dated 1675. Anonymous. Public domain.

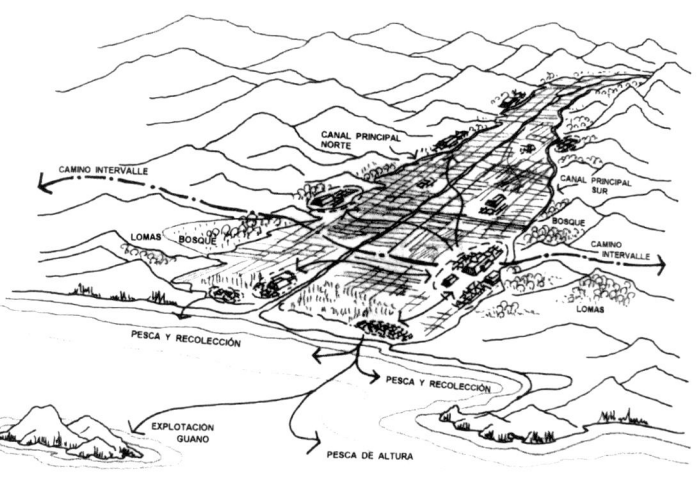

Figure 2. José Canziani; Hypothetical valley of the northern or central coast, illustrating the settlement pattern, with the extension of agricultural management to the medium and lower zones of the valley through the development of irrigation channels in both margins. Source: José Canziani, "Ciudad y territorio". 2009.

soil. These practices reflect a lack of communication between beings, a sense of planning divorced from a tradition of habitation, and constitute precisely what is meant by alienation of the territory from the land.

In the map at figure 2, architect and researcher José Canziani illustrates a hypothetical reconstruction of life in a valley in the ecosystem of the central or northern coast, similar to the site of Lima. In Canziani's map we see that most of the land where the current city stands was allotted to cultivation, and that settlements existed in a more decentralized manner, according to the economic activities of their corresponding areas (fishing, agriculture, politics, etc.). An intervalley path, corresponding with a path known as the Incan road system or *qhapac ñan*, connects all the basins on the coast, facilitating easy exchange between them. From the river derive various irrigation channels that nurture fertile soil in what is now experienced as arid land (Canziani, 2009, 183).

For Canziani, city and territory are coexisting categories, the former a type of "domestication"[10] of the latter. The colonial city, however, is essentially different in that it inaugurates a particular form of unsustainability demanded by a specific economic activity that remains the core of Peruvian economic progress

---

10 José Canziani, "Arquitectura Prehispánica" (course taught at Pontificia Universidad Católica del Perú. April 21 2021).

today: mining for export. The contemporary forms of such export-based economies in South America have been termed neo-extractivism (Gudynas, 2015). In the historical record, extractivism has its roots in a model of accumulation that follows the demands of nascent urban centers in settler colonial societies (Svampa, 2019, 6). In South America, the symbiogenesis of cities and extractivism stands for a single urbanization pattern based on a model of subordination rather than one of reciprocity (Acosta, 2013). Understanding settler colonialism and counter-territorial urban planning as mutually constitutive make the logic of extractivism inseparable from the systems of representation of the colonial city.

Territorial Standpoint   (the future of the watershed)

If we follow the Rímac upwards into the Andes, we reach the district of Huarochirí, where the construction of hydroelectric dams (Huinco and Callahuanca) throughout the twentieth century not only exacerbated the drying of the soil (the subsoils are no longer fed by water vessels[11]), but also failed to bring any resources to the communities that live there. In the official historical record (written in Spanish), Huarochirí is first mentioned in reference to practices of forced

---

11 In particular, *Qochas* and *vasos hídricos*, which are two kinds of wells found in the headwaters. A hydric vase is the smallest well-type system in water sowing, holding up to 10 000 m^3 of water. The *kocha* holds between 10 000 to 100 000 m^3. Cartilla 2. Asociación de Siembra y Cosecha de Agua -ASyCA. Forthcoming.

spiritual indoctrination, marked by the "reductions"[12] of *ayllus* (complex kin-and-town-ships) through the imposition of borders and the burning of the homes and sacred spaces of families that refused to separate (Rosas Cuadros, 1995). The *ayllu* reduction corresponded with the previously mentioned extractivist reconfiguration of labor. The systematic drying of the soil continues, exacerbated by aggressive centralization policies throughout the republican history of Peru that continue to marginalize communities in the Andes. These policies have led to decades of forced migration to coastal cities, especially Lima, where over a third of the country's population lives (Matos Mar, 1984; Gandolfo, 2009).

In the face of these challenges, exacerbated by the disproportionate impact of climate change in the Andean highlands, community leaders resort to territorial approaches to the organization of life, the implementation of which is often challenged by the segmentarist political division of the territory into municipalities (Alencastre, 2021; Magnaghi, 2012). In Huarochirí, the Asociación de Comunidades

---

12 An *ayllu* is a large familial organization constitutive of human, animal, and territorial beings that served as a tributary labor unit in the Inca regime. The reduction of the *ayllus* is the legal term for the forceful separation and extermination of these large, communal families alongside their respective labor practices, and their adaptation into the monogamous Christian model of the nuclear family and its economic activities.

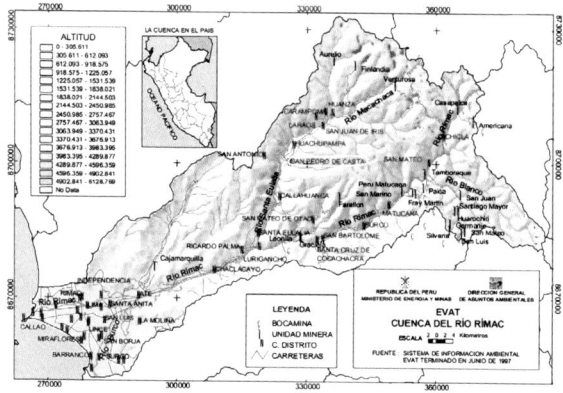

Figure 3. Intervention in a map of the Rímac watershed, running from the Andes to the Pacific Ocean. San Pedro de Casta circled in Yellow by the author. Retrieved from the website of the Ministry of Energy and Mining of Peru: http://www.minem.gob.pe/minem/archivos/file/dgaam/publicaciones/evats/rimac/rimac2.pdf

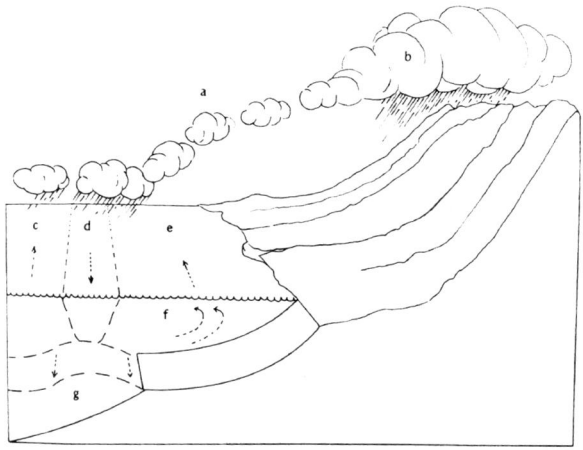

Figure 4. Diagram of the Pacific-facing central Andean ecosystem by Michael Moseley.

Nor-Huarochirí brings together the independent associations of the communities that share the valley of the Santa Eulalia River (which flows into the Rímac). Although striving for territorial organization, the communities of the basin must nevertheless, in most cases, pass requests for funds for the implementation of infrastructure through their corresponding municipalities. Gregorio Ríos founded the Asociación de Comunidades Nor-Huarochirí based on his understanding of a territory closely bound to the movement of water.

While different versions of water sowing and harvesting are, and have been, practiced worldwide, ASyCA's work responds to the ecosystem of the Pacific-facing central Andes. This ecosystem is characterized by having a desert coastline narrowly hemmed in by the Andes. The mountain range rises to over 5000 meters above sea level, a dramatic ascent that generates many neighboring microclimates at different altitudes. The Andes block clouds formed from the evaporation of Pacific Ocean water from reaching the Amazon rainforest, retaining them over the coast year-round. Evaporated ocean water would normally be warm in such a tropical latitude, but in this case the water remains cool because of the cold Humboldt current from the southern seas. As the waters evaporate, they are warmed by

Figure 5. "Water sowing: Forgotten resources and hydric systems" by Gregorio Ríos (Cultura al Agua, 2017)

SIEMBRA DEL AGUA

RECURSOS Y SISTEMAS HIDRICOS OLVIDADOS

ENERO FEBRERO MARZO

1. VASOS
2. CARCAVAS
3. CANALES
4. LAGUNAS
5. HUMEDALES
6. BOFEDALES
7. CRESTAS
8. AMUNAS
9. ZANJAS INFILTRACIÓN
10. FORESTAL – PASTOS
A. VENAS SUBTERRÁNEAS
B. LAGUNAS SUBTERRÁNEAS

OJOS DE AGUAS
PUQUIALES – MANANTIALES
SIN MANTENIMIENTO

the desertic landmass in a temperature inversion that inhibits precipitation until an altitude of about 2500 meters is reached (Moseley, 1974). This happens in the warmer months of the year (November–April) known colloquially, below 2500 meters, as summer and, above 2500 meters, as rain season. The rest of the year, the coast is covered by cool and rainless fog, while the Andes suffer intense drought. The Andean ecosystem, characterized by floods and droughts, has historically demanded sophisticated water management technologies from its inhabitants (Engel, 1980; Canziani, 2009). ASyCA understands water sowing and harvesting as an integral system that brings together most of these technologies in an interdependency.

Walking Listening   (the ways of water)

In the process of writing technical reports for the construction of infrastructure, there is the first moment of diagnosis, which often arises from educational activities where people present their relationships with the project at hand to each other. These are often creative activities, like putting on a play or drawing a map. Social cartography has a long tradition; as a member of ASyCA, my contribution focuses on the practice of field recording, for its unique ability to bring walking and listening together. The mapping process takes the form of intergenerational workshops centered on walking with and listening to the paths of the water. The trajectories of this map are not fixed, as the idea is to start mapping from the ways in which people listen to the movement of water. My role is to offer techniques related to field recording and the facilitation of long sessions of walking and listening, leading to the eventual development of collective forms of archiving the material.

The intent of these workshops is to engage in an acoustic ecology—that is, as Hildegard Westerkamp writes, an "arena" for "the study of the inter-relationship between sound, nature, and society" (Westerkamp, 2002). Westerkamp is a pioneer in the field of acoustic ecology, which emerged from the World Soundscape Project, the work of a group of soundscape composers in British Columbia in the 1970s. By using field recordings of environmental sounds in composition and putting together soundwalks, the group emphasizes listening throughout the composition process. Composition thus becomes about modes of engagement with the environment through sound. While the practice of "soundscape composition" was used from the group's inception, the field of acoustic ecology was only formalized decades later, in the year 2000, with the publication of the first volume of *Soundscape: A Journal of Acoustic Ecology,* edited by Westerkamp herself. Often, soundwalks and field recording sessions are one and the same, and this interrelation of walking and listening in soundscape composition is a focus of the work this paper relates to. In the field of sound studies, 'soundscape' refers to a specific legacy, heavily influenced by a 1976 book by R. Murray Schafer: *On Sonic Environment and The Soundscape: The Tuning of the World*. Many critiques of Schafer (a colleague of Westerkamp) have emerged since then. Tim Ingold argues against Schafer's transposition of the visual mechanics of the landscape into sound, claiming that this results in basing ideas in the same binaries that gave them birth—ideas that many in the field of visual culture have long tried to undo (Ingold, 2007). Namely, and chiefly, framing things in terms of "the relation between man and the sounds of his environment" (Schafer, 1967, 3) already presupposes a problematic division between the human and the natural. The proposal made here for a sonic map aims to de-center this explicitly gendered (and implicitly racialized) separation of human subjectivity, imbued in the practice of soundscape composition, in accordance with Ana María Ochoa's assertion about the influence of post-structuralist anthropology in sound studies:

> This is not an issue of how to "include" the human in the environment but rather of asking how the given and the made are conceptualized and thereby related to the reformulation of notions of production, habitation, the acoustic, and form. (Ochoa, 2016, 132)

When recording in the field, headphones can be used to hear what is being recorded as it happens. This state of amplified hearing informs movement on-site in particular ways. Paying attention to the challenges and potentials of walking with recorder in hand not only offers mobility, but also makes the physical presence of a body an unavoidable part of the recording (the movement of the headphone cable, friction from clothing, footsteps on soil and stones, breath sounds that indicate the pace of the body, and so on.) A "masterful" approach to field recording would demand that these mentioned traces should disappear, in order to maintain a seamless aesthetic flow of "environmental" sounds, separate from any indication of the recording human. Mastery would mean using a handle or a tripod and a windscreen on the microphone, so that nothing that reaches it does so without a filter. In a gesture of mastery of non-mastery (Taussig, 2021), the workshops encourage experimentation with movement-based approaches as a way of understanding that, in recording, the operator too becomes record. Embracing the interruptions of touch and motion, of breathing and walking, creatively, is a way to begin to suspend the separation of the given and the made, understanding gesticulations, sensibilities, the archive, and the territory as mutually constitutive.

Water sowing and harvesting are studied by walking up to the mountain peaks and following the descending paths of the water, learning how to read the inscriptions in the soil and stones, the traces of dams, channels, and caves. In proposing to connect with this practice through sonic mapping, listening takes place in motion, by walking while recording as a way of mapping the space from within–cartography from habitation.

Walking as a critical practice also has a history as a discipline. The activity is usually approached from a perspective of labor, and in reference to urban spaces (rural spaces tend to work by contrast.) Walking in a city is associated with the incorporation of a set of standard disciplines (posture, pace, clear direction) that follow a productivist logic of reproduction (Ingold and Vergunst, 2008, 2). In contrast, critical walking practices focus on play or other dimensions of labor that refuse this logic. Key examples are the figure of the *flâneur* (Benjamin, 1999) and the practice of the *dérive* (Debord, 1956)–what Francesco Careri, in his influential book *Walkscapes: Walking as an Aesthetic Practice*, refers to as the "anti-walk." For Careri, the issue at hand is "the communication of the experience in aesthetic form." (Careri, 2002, 207), thus critical walking is framed as always bound to the duty of counter-hegemonic forms of mapping.

In working with Asociación de Siembra y Cosecha de Agua, the intervention of sonic cartography proposed emphasizes the interconnectedness of habitation, mapping, archiving, and constructing. The aesthetic experience of amplified hearing opens channels of communication with the territory. A dimension of this is made reproducible[13] by field recording, and is accordingly available to be shared for collective study. The methods of editing, formatting, and ordering the recordings, alongside communication of the experience of recording constitute the map, which stands as an archive that has the capacity to directly inform the shape of the infrastructure to be built.

Concluding Offer   (An active line on a walk[14])

Maps are made of lines. With sound, this materializes quite literally in the timeline. A single field recording is a line in time, a trajectory walked, with its chances and choices. The sonic map begins when bringing these walks together. Last April, members

---

13 As Westerkamp remarks, there is a clear difference between what the microphone records and what the ears listen to. This suggests that only one dimension is reproducible, and that this dimension is unique to its own condition of reproducibility.

14 Quote from Paul Klee. See: Klee, Paul. 1968. *Pedagogical Sketchbooks*. Translated by Sibyl Moholy-Nagy. London: Faber and Faber,

of the Asociación de Siembra y Cosecha de Agua went up to San Pedro de Casta on a recording trip. The purpose was to record with GPS precision the infrastructure for water sowing that the community had built the year before, as well as the infrastructure for water harvesting that is yet to be built. The GPS points were accompanied by photographic records to which I proposed a sonic complement. The first day was spent in Marcahuasi, a complex of impressive pre-Columbian stonework in the highest peaks of the mountain, where community members enclosed naturally formed depressions with dams made of stone and adobe (remains of which are present from pre-Columbian times). The recording trip was right at the end of the rain season, so the depressions were filled with rainwater to a considerable degree of their capacity.

To conclude this article, I offer a line from the recording trip, edited together with minimal overlaps that give a sense of continuity, as well as rough cuts and examples of in-recorder leveling, presenting them in the condition of edited fragments of an archive. Listeners will hear my breath and steps, and the friction of my body as well as gusts of wind hitting the microphone. The words of my collaborators, learning as we go, and the sounds of the machines

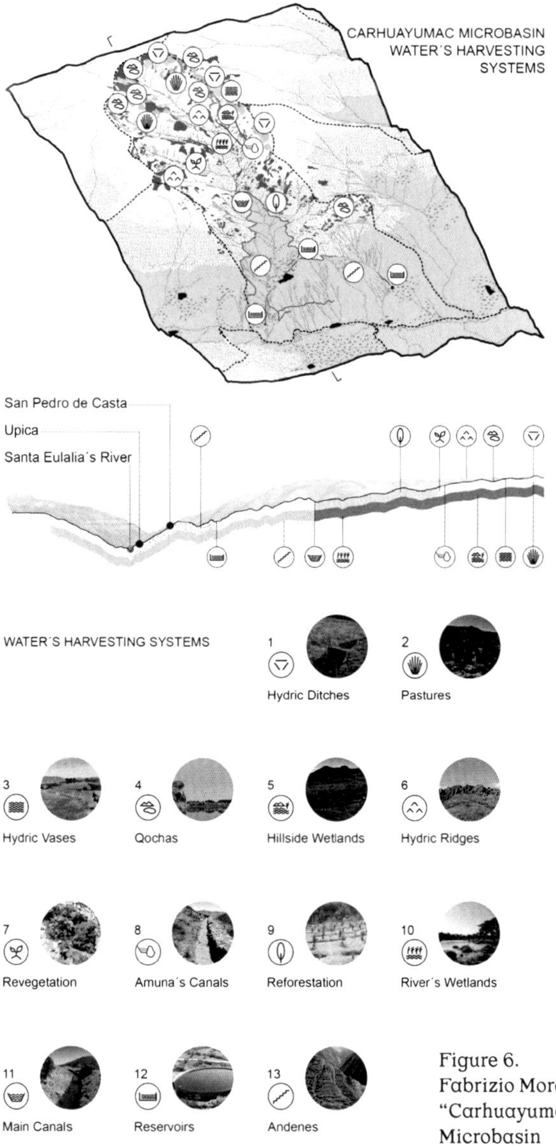

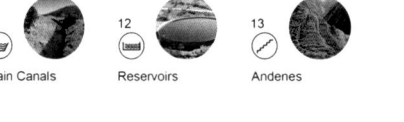

Figure 6. Fabrizio Mora, "Carhuayumac Microbasin Water Harvesting Systems", 2021.

as they record the names of the bodies of water, the height of the dams, and the time of the day are heard. For those who were present, these recordings are remarkable memory aids, giving a visceral as well as technical sense of what it was like to walk down the paths of the water. They become a living archive, linking our movements to those of the hydrological system. The water, in the beginning, is nowhere to be heard, as the walk started amid the *qochas* and smaller wells, where water is either still or infiltrates deep underground. The silence is of the water (Fantinato, 2021). What is heard is the movement around it, of birds gathering, of small organisms breathing in the shallows, of humans mapping and walking and talking. As our path descends, the water infiltrates the recording with its motion, dripping and running through underground channels and overground streams.

What is left is to share. To keep walking and listening to the ways of water sowing and harvesting. To sustain the living archive that is latent in the territory.

Audio 1. Vered Engelhard, "Line with ASyCA, Marcahuasi, 17/04/21", 2021.

References

Cartilla 2. Asociación de Siembra y Cosecha de Agua - ASyCA. Forthcoming.

Acosta, Alberto. 2013. "Extractivism and neo-extractivism: two sides of the same curse." in Beyond Development. Alternative Visions from Latin America. *Permanent Working Group on Alternative to Development*, edited by Lang, Miriam and Dunia Mokrani ,. Luxembourg, Netherlands: Transnational Institute Luxembourg – Rosa Foundation.

Andrés Alencastre. "El enfoque territorial en los programas de siembra y cosecha de agua" (Conference paper presented at *Conversatorio de Siembra y Cosecha de Agua*. Lima, CEDEP – PERU Centro de Estudios para el Desarrollo y la Participación. June 17 2021).

Benjamin, Walter. 1999. *The Arcades Project*. Translated by Howard Eiland and Kevin Mclaughlin. Cambridge: The Belknap Press of Harvard University Press.

Canziani Amico, José. 2009. *Ciudad y territorio en los Andes* : contribuciones a la historia del urbanismo prehispánico. Lima: Pontificia Universidad Católica del Perú.

Careri, Francesco. 2002. *Walkscapes: Walking as Aesthetic Practice*. Barcelona, Mexico, Portugal: Editorial Gustavo Gil.

Debord, Guy. 1956. *Theory of the Dérive*. Translated by Ken Knabb. Available at Situationist International Online.

De la Cadena, Marisol. 2015. *Earth Beings: Ecologies of Practice across Andean Worlds* Durham: Duke University Press.

del Castillo, Juan Manuel. "Lima la fértil: De la inconsistencia del discurso de la ciudad-desierto" *Archdaily*. August 5, 2016. (https://www.archdaily.pe/pe/792779/lima-la-fertil-de-la-inconsistencia-del-discurso-de-la-ciudad-desierto?fbclid=IwAR-03h4_4OSnWDlfwsQa-07Utqac6XWphO3eDUctl_AiDYHKEaRvKyexxzoUg).

Engel, Friederick. 1980. *Prehistoric Andean Ecology: Man, Settlement and Environment in the Andes*. New York: Hunter College.

Gandolfo, Daniella. 2009. *The City at its Limits: Taboo, Transgression, and Urban Renewal in Lima*. Chicago: University of Chicago Press.

Géo de Siqueira, Maria Fantinato. "Resonances of Land: Silence, Noise, and Extractivism in the Brazilian Amazon" (PhD dissertation, Columbia University, 2021).

Gudynas, Eduardo. 2015. *Extr activismos: Ecología, econ omía y política de un modo de entender eldesarrollo y la Naturaleza*. Cochabamba: Centro de Documentación e Información Bolivia.

Ingold, Tim. 2007. "Against soundscape" in *Autumn leaves: sound and the environment in artistic practice,* edited by A. Carlyle. Paris: Double Entendre.

Ingold, Tim and Jo Lee Vergunst. 2008. "Introduction" in *Ways of Walking: Ethnography and Practice on Foot. Edited by* Ingold and Vergunst. Burlington: Ashgate Publishing Limited.

Kaulicke, Peter. 2008. "*La economía en el período formativo*" in Economía Prehispánica, Tomo I edited by Waldemar Espinoza, Luis G. Lumbreras, Peter Kaulicke, & Julián I. Santillana, 208-212. Lima: Banco Central de Reserva del Perú .

Klee, Paul. 1968. *Pedagogical Sketchbooks*. Translated by Sibyl Moholy-Nagy. London: Faber and Faber.

Magnaghi, Alberto. 2012. "The Role of Historical Rural Landscapes in Territorial Planning". *Environmental History:* 131-39.

Matos Mar, José. 1984. *Desborde popular y crisis del estado*. Lima: Instituto de Estudios Peruanos.

Mora Sansotta, Fabrizio. "Estructura del Paisaje: Siembra y Cosecha de Agua en San Pedro de Casta" (Thesis for B.Arch., Pontificia Universidad Católica del Perú, 2020)

Moseley, Michael E. 1975. *Maritime Foundations in Andean Civilization*. Menlo Park: Cummings Publishing Company.

Nixon, Rob. 2011. *Slow Violence and the Environmentalism of the Poor*. Cambridge: Harvard University Press.

Ochoa Gautier, Ana M. 2016. "Acoustic Multiculturalism" in *Boundary 2*, vol 43, issue 1 *(*February). Durham: Duke University Press.

Rosas Cuadros, Emilio E. 1995. *La Provincia de Huarochirí en la Historia: Coloniaje e Independencia*. Lima: [¿San Marcos?].

Rostworowski, Maria. 1981. *Recursos naturales renovables y pesca, siglos XVI y XVII*. Lima: Instituto de Estudios Peruanos.

Sletto, Bjorn. Bryan, Joe. Torrado, Marla. Hale, Charles. Barry, Deborah. 2013. "Territoriality, Participatory Mapping, and Natural Resources Policy: The Latin American Experience" in *Cuadernos de geografía*, Volume 22, Issue 2:193.

Schafer, Murray. 1976. *On Sonic Environment and The Soundscape: The Tuning of the World*. Rochester: Destiny Books.

Svampa, Maristela. 2019. *Neo-Extractivism in Latin America: Socio-environmental Conflicts, the Territorial Turn, and New Political Narratives*. Cambridge: Cambridge University Press.

Taussig, Michael. 2020. *Mastery of Non-mastery in the Age of Meltdown*. Chicago: The University of Chicago Press.

Tsing, Anna. 2015. *The Mushroom at the End of the World: On the Possibility of Life in Capitalist Ruins*. Princeton and Oxford: Princeton University Press

Westerkamp, Hildegard. 2000. "Editorial." *Soundscape: The Journal of Acoustic Ecology* 1, no. 1.

Westerkamp, Hildegard. 2002. "Linking Soundscape Composition and Acoustic Ecology" in *Organized Sound, An International Journal of Music and Technology*, Volume 7, Number 1.

Wynter, Sylvia. 1995. "1492: A New World View" in, *Race, Discourse, and the Origin of the Americas: A New World View*, edited by Lawrence Hyatt, Vera and Rex Nettleford. Washington and London: Smithsonian Institute Press

Resounding Epistemologies of Conflict: Auralities in Colombia's Historical Memory

ANA RUIZ VALENCIA is a Colombian curator, musician and researcher, interested in contemporary artistic practices, particularly those related to aural culture, philosophy and politics of sound. As a violinist, her work focuses on experimental music and improvisation, frequently collaborating with musicians, writers and artists in Colombia and abroad. Ruiz Valencia co-authored *Charles Fréger – Cimarrón: Freedom and Masquerade* (Thames & Hudson, 2019) and was part of the curatorial team at the *45 Salón Nacional de Artistas* in Colombia. Ruiz Valencia currently serves as curator at the Universidad de Antioquia's Museum, MUUA and Auditum Festival in Medellín, Colombia.

> The situation here is intense; we're surrounded by M-19 personnel. Please cease fire immediately! Let the public hear this, this is urgent—it's life or death. Can you hear me? [...] The President of the Republic needs to give the order to cease fire right now![1]
>
> — Alfonso Reyes Echandía, *Broadcast on National Radio*

The bloody conflict that has taken place in Colombia throughout the 20th and 21st centuries is partially a consequence of civil wars inherited from the nineteenth century and partially the result of the conflicts of the colonial period. The combination of a colonial caste system that established a social and hierarchical racial order, classifying people according to their proportion of Spanish blood, the struggle for territorial and political control of the nascent republic by elites from different regions of the country and, in recent decades, the so-called war on drugs, have produced structures of exclusion that result in a breeding ground for internal conflict and political instability. This article focuses on the aural memory related to certain historical events and processes. It then addresses ways in which contemporary artists have used sound, as both strategy and material for resisting and deconstructing metanarratives,

---

1 Reyes Echandía, president of the Supreme Court of Colombia, asks for help on a phone call broadcast live on National Radio as the Palace of Justice was occupied by the M-19 guerrilla group and bombed by Colombian military forces, with nearly 350 hostages held inside.

and the practice of listening as a political act, in the creation of other possible worlds. The aural component of Colombian conflict is understood here from various perspectives: the construction of memory through mass media such as radio, the use of audio recordings in the clarification of truth, testimony and subjective narration as an aspect of symbolic reparations, and works of art that question official narratives, contrasting hegemonic and subordinate horizons of meaning to reveal intersubjective realities.

Act I.

Radio has played a significant role in modern Colombian history, but I will focus on two key events: The Bogotazo uprising (1948) and the Palace of Justice siege (1985).

On April 9, 1948, the radio played a central role in a popular uprising incited by the assassination of Jorge Eliécer Gaitán, a left-wing political leader and presidential candidate for the Liberal Party. The uprising led to hundreds of deaths and the destruction of a significant part of downtown Bogotá[2]. It may have been the first time that radio connected all

---

[2] The "Bogotazo" took place while Bogotá celebrated the 9th Pan-American Conference, which took place from March 30 to May 2, 1948. Among the most far-reaching of the issues discussed were the adoption of the Organizing Constitution of the American States; the American Treaty on Peaceful Solutions (or "Bogotá Pact"), and the American Declaration of the Rights and Responsibilities of Man.

Colombians around a single event: Liberal leaders from the Junta Central Revolucionaria de Gobierno (Central Revolutionary Government Junta) broke into the National Broadcaster, took microphones away from journalists, and called for the insubordination of government forces all over Colombia. Radio broadcasters from downtown Bogotá reported on the events with ire; all over the country, the news spread like wildfire through local and underground broadcasters. Using hand-made equipment, they informed the public about current events while encouraging resistance, coordinating attacks on institutions, and reporting dubious revolutionary victories across the airwaves:

Listen:

Audio 1. Radiodifusora Nacional - Transmisión 9/Abril/1948.

Audio 2. Registro Sonoro 11 - Toma De La Radio Nacional - 09 De Abril 1948.

Revolutionary and leftist forces of Colombia, the revolution carries the day in Cali and Medellin. It carries the day in Barranquilla. Leftist forces have taken over the government in the capital of Atlántico [...]

From Corinto, from Puerto Tejada, from every place along the eastern Cauca Valley, from the south, to bring about a victorious revolution [...] Liberals, take up all of your positions, and all of your employees or workers who can use a weapon must make them available, in the service of the people.

A liberal from Boyacá speaks to the people of Boyacá who have been the first victims of the slogans of blood and fire [...] I want the provinces of Santander to be alert and stand guard, to arm all the men of the countryside, to find money and put together a revolution.[3]

---

[3] Transcriptions (originally in Spanish) of *Transformaciones de la radio en Colombia* ("Transformations of Radio in Colombia"), by María del Pilar Chaves Castro, based on radio archives stored in the National Sound Archive.

Figure 1. Radio espectros. Courtesy of Leonel Vásquez.

Radio espectros (Radio Spectrums), (2013), by the Colombian sound artist Leonel Vásquez, is a bicycle-drawn, travelling radio device that takes over the frequency of the Colombian National Broadcaster and plays recorded radio broadcasts from April 9, 10 and 11, 1948, interspersed with music and radio dramas from the period. Vásquez reinterpreted and activated archival audio from the National Sound Archive by creating situations for it to be listened to in public spaces, such as parks and streets. Words are not the only important element of the sonic message visitors listen to: in addition to the energy and alarm heard in the agitated voices, attention is paid to environmental sounds, and to the glitches generated by low-quality transmissions and their eventual recording onto a physical medium.

The work is based on the notion of sound as a physical and public space, limited by the state's policies for bandwidth allocation. The events of April 1948 revealed the power of radio in processes of popular uprising and the state's inability to control radio bandwidth. These "pirate" radio stations played a central role in popular organization and had both direct and indirect impact on the armed mobilization that followed. After the Bogotazo, a series of reforms limited bandwidth access to transmitters (like community or amateur broadcasters) that were not connected to a business structure, making access subject to prevailing power structures.

Thirty-seven years later, in 1985, the radio broadcast across the entire country the pleas of Alfonso Reyes Echandía, president of the Supreme Court of Colombia, as he spoke from a telephone under his desk in the Palace of Justice while gunshots were heard in the background[4]. That November 6, bus drivers in Bogota turned up the volume on their radios as their passengers listened with surprise, while the families of those who worked in the headquarters of the Supreme Court followed the events, minute by minute, from their homes. A few hours earlier, the M-19 guerilla group had entered the building and taken the magistrates, workers, and visitors hostage. Now, the army and the police surrounded the

---

4 Listen:

building and were beginning an operation to retake it, which would last until the next day. The process of retaking the building left nearly a hundred dead, including civilians, armed forces, and guerilla fighters, and at least eleven missing persons, whose disappearances remain unresolved.

The demands of the M-19 guerillas included the right to a daily television spot or an hour per day on the national radio. Meanwhile, the radio stations broadcast live calls from hostages inside the Palace. The broadcast audio is multidimensional: not only are the interviewees' voices heard in the foreground, but the voices of the guerillas, echoing bursts of gunfire, and explosions are also heard in the background. Time is an important dimension too. As the day wears on, the conversations become more agitated, the gunshots louder, and pleading voices are heard shouting, "Don't shoot!"[5]

---

5 Some radio excerpts from this period can be heard at:
Terror en el Palacio de Justicia (Terror in the Palace of Justice) by Caracol Radio: https://caracol.com.co/radio/2020/11/03/podcast/1604437581_068114.html

La noche más larga (The Longest Night) by Radio Ambulante:
https://radioambulante.org/audio/la-noche-mas-larga-1
https://radioambulante.org/audio/la-noche-mas-larga-parte-2

Palacio de Justicia: El día que silenciaron la radio (Palace of Justice: The day they silenced the radio) by Revista Semana: https://www.semana.com/nacion/articulo/palacio-de-justicia-30-anos-el-dia-que-silenciaron-la-radio/448160-3/

Towards the end of the first day, the country's main radio stations received a call from Noemí Sanín, then the Communications Minister, ordering them to interrupt their transmissions and broadcast a soccer match instead. Yamid Amat, director of the Caracol station, said that he would follow the order if other broadcasters did the same. The minister replied that if he did not interrupt his transmission, she would order the army to take over the station and turn off the transmitters. Also interesting are the actions of Pablo Montaña, a blind musician and radio aficionado who lived just a few blocks from the Palace. Using a walkie-talkie, Montaña intercepted conversations between the military commanders of the operation to retake the Palace and, realizing that these contained important information, recorded several cassettes until noon on November 7.

Figure 2. Script for *Llamado de guerra*. Courtesy of the artist.

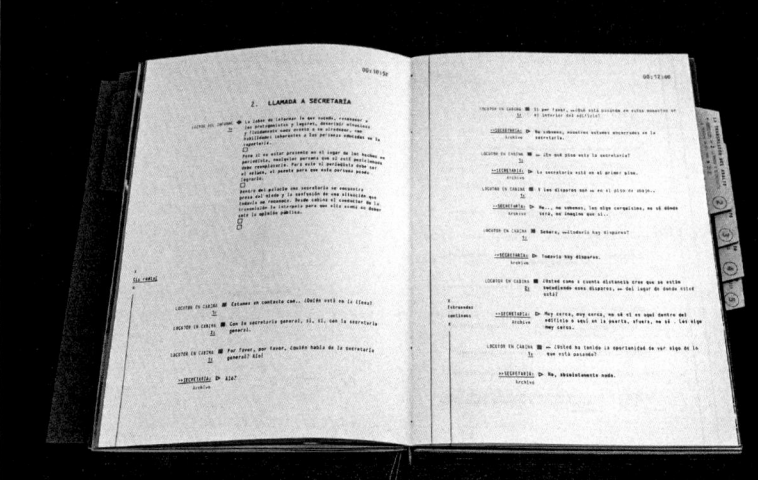

Llamado de guerra: archivo sonoro del conflicto (Call of War: An Audio Archive of the Conflict), by Esteban Ferro, is an archive of key moments in the political conflicts of Latin America in which radio and audio recordings played an important role. In 2019, Ferro addressed three events in Colombian history: the Leticia Incident of 1932, the assassination of Jorge Eliécer Gaitán, and the Palace of Justice siege[6]. Including both fiction and non-fiction, the project investigates mediatization (re)produced by radio reporting, based on an analysis of the influence these have on the development of the events they report. The archive recreates these processes in a series of transmissions, performances, listening sessions and print publications.

To Ferro, the difficulty of obtaining the rights to reproduce original audio recordings became an opportunity to understand how media discourse (in this case radio) is built through production strategies that include the creation of scripts, the broadcast of live interviews and soundscapes, and the use of sound effects, Foley sounds, music, and both live and pre-recorded sound design techniques. In this context, three aspects of production are especially interesting: the construction of a fictional narrative based on reenactment, the

---

6 Listen:

Figure 3. *Llamado de guerra*. One person manages the archival audio, three speakers, and improvised environmental sounds provided by fellow artist Ángela Marciales. Photograph courtesy of Esteban Ferro.

development of a script/score in which the analysis of radio stories is translated into a series of notations, and the final performative-sonic action *per se*, which involves a combination of archival material, incidental sounds, constructed texts and live speech. Performers bring the past and present together by interacting with "dead" voices from the original recordings and including elements related to the present, such as vuvuzelas in the soccer match section.

Both Ferro and Vásquez use archival audio recordings to problematize the medium of radio as an agent in historical processes, deconstructing sonic narratives through a mixture of fiction and non-fiction, and demanding active listening from the public.

According to Jesús Martín-Barbero (1993), mediations are a "place" where it is possible to understand the interaction between the space of production and that of reception. They are non-dualistic communication processes—ever-evolving interactions between the media and the listeners, with political and cultural implications.

Radio is a field of power relations during conflicts: whoever is in charge can project a specific message and influence the listeners' emotions about a certain situation. Like other mass media outlets, radio reproduces ideas and feelings that help in defining both collective identities and intersubjective realities. However, as historical events develop, listeners construct a subjective existence in relation to those events that also exert an influence on subsequent discursive outputs by mass media.

Act II.

Stories related to systematic violence, such as displacement, massacres or forced disappearance, are sometimes recorded not by mass media outlets, but as part of criminal court cases, transitional justice, or symbolic reparations. Between 1977 and 2015, at least 60,630 people were victims of enforced disappearance[7] in Colombia[8]. By 2018, Colombia had registered 7.7 million victims of forced displacement[9], making it the country with the highest number of displaced persons in the world, according to the United Nations High Commissioner for Refugees (UNHCR, or ACNUR in Spanish-speaking countries). In 2020 alone, 76 massacres accounted for 292 deaths (UN, 2021).

In the artist María Alejandra Ordóñez's sound installation *Retratos no hablados* (Unspoken Portraits), exhibited in Bogotá at the Center for Memory, Peace and Reconciliation in 2016, visitors answer telephones that ring randomly and reproduce intimate stories about the mourning of close friends or

---

7 According to the Declaration on the Protection of All Persons from Enforced Disappearance, enforced disappearance occurs when "persons are arrested, detained or abducted against their will or otherwise deprived of their liberty by officials of different branches or levels of Government, or by organized groups or private individuals acting on behalf of, or with the support, direct or indirect, consent or acquiescence of the Government." UN General Assembly, Resolution 47/133, (18 December, 1992).

8 Centro Nacional de Memoria Histórica. 2016. "Hasta encontrarlos: el drama de la desaparición forzada en Colombia". https://centrodememoriahistorica.gov.co/descargas/informes2016/hasta-encontrarlos/hasta-encontrarlos-drama-de-la-desaparicion-forzada-en-colombia.pdf

9 The International Organization for Migration defines a forced migrant as any person migrating to "escape persecution, conflict, repression, natural and human-made disasters, ecological degradation, or other situations that endanger their lives, freedom or livelihood".

relatives of the disappeared. Ordóñez's interest is "to problematize the concept of disappearances from its different semantic possibilities, as well as a strategy of concealment of the intentions, facts and ways in which the conflict was narrated" (Akil, 2019).

The use of telephones creates a close relationship between the listener and the victim while also establishing distance by means of the impossibility of responding to the message heard. The selection of the telephone as an object also connects with the artist's memories—her grandfather asked his family to ensure the line was always open, in case a phone call from the artist's uncle, one of the disappeared, was received.

Paisajes invisibles (Invisible Landscapes), by Colectivo Radiolaboratorio (Mauricio Prieto and Sandra Jaramillo), was a mobile and collapsible structure comprising of a bicycle-like vehicle that transported plastic tubes that were then installed in public spaces to delineate a space in which passers-by were interviewed by the artists with microphones, recorders, and a speaker. Between 2016 and 2017, this temporary, participatory installation travelled to plazas in Cali, Bogotá and Medellín (the main arrival points for displaced persons). Supported by local organizations, the project invited visitors to think about soundmarks from the places they were

Figure 4. *Paisajes invisibles*. Photograph courtesy of Mauricio Prieto.

displaced from, and then imitate or describe them, so that these memories could be recreated, remixed, and amplified by the artists. The project was based on the idea that a landscape can be narrated, recalled, and reconstructed through oral histories, despite being vacated or having ceased to exist due to conflict. *Paisajes invisibles* was organized around a mechanism for editing and publishing audio material, the insertion of which into public spaces aimed to bring people together to exchange memories and replay the resulting soundscapes. Radiolaboratorio defined their project as an "open museography" because it evolves as it encounters the dynamics of a place in dispute, its size is adaptable, and the soundscapes that are both created and reproduced at the installation are enriched in every new place it inhabits.

The sound installations *El canto de los yarumos* (The Song of the Yarumos), (2015) and *Cantos silentes en cuerpos de madera* (Silent Songs in Wooden Bodies), (2017), by Leonel Vásquez, use voice recordings, soundscapes, and the chants of victims' relatives to stress listening as a political act and as a central part of the dialogue surrounding reconciliation and symbolic reparations.

The first piece was installed in the three yarumo trees (*Cecropia peltata*) planted by victims at the Bogotá Center for Memory, Peace and Reconciliation (known as CMPR, from its initials in Spanish), while the second work was created in Santo Domingo (in

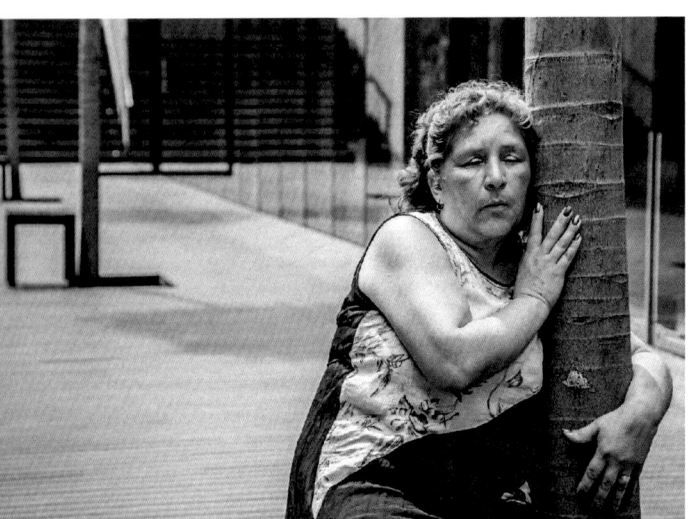

Figure 5. *El canto de los yarumos*. Photograph courtesy of Leonel Vásquez.

the department of Arauca) as part of the symbolic reparations after the government was condemned by the Inter-American Court of Human Rights for the massacre it perpetrated against this community. In both cases, Vásquez relates corporeal and tactile experience by placing transducers on the roots of the trees, using the mechanical conduction of sound through the tree trunks to propose a form of listening based on physical contact. At the CMPR, the artist installed chairs next to the yarumos, which subtly interrupted the quotidian nature of the space and made it so that, when visitors casually took a seat, they began to feel the sounds that vibrated through the trees. Both works took as their jumping-off point questions of what we should learn from these events, what to say to someone who might want to reconnect with these experiences and the messages behind them. The answers, made up of poems, songs, and stories, proposed a close and personal relationship with the listener.

The anti-monumental and the notion of intimacy are key ideas within the works by Ordóñez, Radiolaboratorio, and Vásquez mentioned above: Both Vásquez and Radiolaboratorio emphasize the anti-monumental as a fundamental axis for working in spaces of collective mourning, with listening as a multidimensional experience that implies temporal, corporeal, tactile, and emotional layers. These installations dialogue with the physical and social space they inhabit. Additionally, they recognize a difference between subjective memory and the ideal of truth in processes of reconciliation. All these works understand Memory as a subjective process based on open stories—non-definitive and created in direct dialogue with victims. Radiolaboratorio uses temporary, pop-up actions in public spaces, while Vásquez boosts the symbolic meaning of materials and places, creating subtle and intimate listening experiences that go beyond the acousmatic and recognize them as tactile-body experiences. Intimacy is also fundamental for Ordóñez, although explored from a nostalgic perspective and from the bodily experience emerging from an interaction with certain types of telephones (mostly those commonly used in the nineties).

Act III.

Carlos Castro and Fabio Melecio Palacios are artists whose works connect the violence of the colonial past with contemporary processes of exclusion. Rooted in a colonial caste system that established a social and hierarchical racial order, contemporary Colombia continues to deal with classism and racism inherited from the colonial era.

An important part of Carlos Castro's oeuvre comes from the resignification of objects loaded with trauma. In 2013, Castro took inspiration from the confluence of three powers within the history of Colombia: the state, the church and drug traffickers. Right next to each other, in the borough of Los Mártires, stands the Basilica of the National Vow (Voto Nacional)[10], the Headquarters of the National Army's Recruiting Command, and the "Bronx," the city's main illicit drug dispensary. The installation took place a few blocks away, in the colonial era church of Santa Clara, today a museum.

Capilla blanca (White Chapel), (2013) is a police squad car that replicates the interior decor of the church. In an experience that sits somewhere between claustrophobia and confessional, each visitor is "captured" for several minutes in the car in a sonic ambiance that integrates radio broadcasts, religious sounds (such as the Angelus), melodies from the military bands that play at certain times of day next to the church, plus a violent sound of knocking in the car.

Colombia is a predominantly Catholic country consecrated to the Sacred Heart of Jesus, a devotional image of Jesus that refers to the metaphor of

---

[10] Construction on the Basilica began in 1902, to honor the Sacred Heart of Jesus, in the hope that building the church would help to create peace between Liberals and Conservatives during the Thousand Days' War.

Figure 6. Capilla blanca. Photograph courtesy of Carlos Castro.

suffering and sacrifice. *Potencias* (Powers), (2013), part of the *Legiones* (Legions) series, features knives made by hand, using found materials such as rubber, wire or glass, that have been confiscated by the police. The artist uses these knives to build melodic percussion instruments, in which each knife plays an individual note in religious songs such as "Sagrado corazón en vos confío" (Sacred Heart in you I Trust) or "Tu reinarás" (You will reign). The name *Potencias*, derived from the religious iconography inherited from the colonial period, is taken from the Catholic argot that refers to the three golden flames placed on the sacred heart of Jesus. Castro updates the meaning of these melodies by contrasting them with handmade knives that are the only means of defense for those who are not protected by the police, the state or the dominant religion.

Raíz (Root) follows a similar strategy to *Potencias*, although using a melody of indigenous origins found by the artist's brother and collaborator in *Les Flûtes Indiennes d'Amérique du Sud*, a French compilation of melodies from different South American countries. Two sound sculptures are built out of *basuco* pipes (used for smoking unrefined coca-paste, some decommissioned, others bought by the artist directly from users) that revolve around a motor that emits puffs of air. This movement produces an earthy sound that recalls Andean wind instruments like the *quena* or the *siku*, while outlining the ritual melody "Nos Cedron" (composer unknown).

Placing this sound sculpture in the church provides a reading of the colonial power imposed on ancestral cultures that resulted in their eradication, removal from the public visibility, obscurity, and marginalization, and subjected the indigenous population to processes of urban, political, social, and cultural exclusion. Furthermore, the relationship between the sound produced by *basuco* pipes and the Andean melodies and timbres evoked speaks to the process of profaning coca, a sacred plant for various native cultures, progressively transformed and degraded into cocaine and *basuco* (coca paste).

Figure 7. *Potencias*. Photograph courtesy of Carlos Castro.

Figure 8. *Raíz*. Photograph courtesy of Carlos Castro.

The word "instrument" may be key to interpreting Castro's works: the musical instrument, weapons as instruments of defense and protection, the instrument for consuming narcotics and, in a wider sense, religion, war, the police, the state, and music itself as instruments of domestication, persecution, marginalization, or oppression.

The work of Fabio Melecio Palacios is also related to long-term processes, defined by a particular geographic, historical, and social context. Fabio was born in Barbacoas, Nariño but moved as a young child to San Antonio, Valle del Cauca when his father found employment as a sugar cane harvester at the Central Castilla mill.

Valle del Cauca is known for its extensive sugar mills. This industry is rooted in colonial *haciendas*, with their production originally based on slave labor. Since at least the seventeenth century, the ownership and accumulation of land in the Valle del Cauca region has been concentrated primarily in the hands of the descendants of colonial settlers, as a direct consequence of the looting of indigenous societies that occurred during the colonial period. From the nineteenth century onwards, the social pyramid continued to be dominated by the landowners, while the material base of society passed from enslaved labor to the work of peons and tenants, combining the old colonial structure with other pseudo-bourgeois elements, in a process that slightly improved work conditions over time.[11]

In the 1980s, the reapers of Palacios' father's generation were hired directly by companies that provided benefits for their families. However, when the 1991 Constitution came into effect, with Colombia's entrance into the global neoliberal system, new social relations of production—such as the concept of external hiring—came about, leading to precariousness of employment, deregulation and reduction of rural salaries (Castillo & Castaño, 2021). Contracts were shortened, workers had no guarantee of being hired again every year, and previous benefits such as paid school for workers' children were lost. This change notably worsened conditions for reapers, who lost job stability and the certainty of pensions upon retirement.

Palacios' sound installation from 2011, *BMR (Bamba, Martillo y Refilón)*,[12] emerges from a desire to pay homage to his father and vindicate his labor as

---

11 See: Mejía Prado, E., A. Montayo Urrutia. 1987. "Origen y formación del ingenio azucarero industrializado en el Valle del Cauca." *Historia y Espacio - Revista de Estudios Históricos Regionales*, XI-XII: 55-107.

12 *Bamba, martillo* and *refilón* are types of machetes used by reapers in the immense sugar-cane fields of the Cauca Valley.

Figure 9. *BMR*. Photograph courtesy of Fabio Melecio Palacio.

Figure 10. In a nearly ritual procedure, each reaper puts a red, brushed-cotton cloth on his leg, grabs the machete and puts on his protector. Photograph courtesy of Fabio Melecio Palacios.

a sugar cane reaper. *BMR* and a previous piece, *Bamba 45*, are based on the everyday, personal act of sharpening a machete.

In *BMR*, 582 machetes hang from the ceiling, at a height that nearly brushes against the heads of visitors. A bright, repetitive, metallic, echoing sound of blades is reproduced in the space to reinforce the threat they pose to those who pass under the machetes and smell the soot from the burnt cane that comes from their old blades. This sound is a recording of the *in-situ* performance of three reapers sharpening their machetes—among them the artist's father—and who seem to maintain a pace with the metallic clang of their blades as they knock off the soot every so often. Although it doesn't belong specifically to a musical piece, this ritual does have melody and rhythm, and these turn into a kind of mantra as they repeat, over and over, in the room.

> It's those things that weigh on you, that sometimes you can't knock down, take off or get rid of. From the reaper's perspective, there are the working conditions: they have their tools, but the issue of hiring, their day to day, their way of living together in the same space, their cultural life, their identity is constantly under threat. That's where the idea of entering a space where you feel threatened comes from. [...] I thought that there was a performative action [in the act of sharpening the machete]. [...] It becomes a nearly silent act: there is no voice, but there is the sound of a tool. That's where I feel there is strength, in the cries of those who are gone, but the noise remains in the ear, in the mind. Each time

you hear the sound of sharpening, there is an act of remembering. (Fabio Melecio Palacios, personal correspondence, 2021)

In contrast to the sounds of *BMR*, which were recorded by only three reapers, in *Bamba 45* (presented in Cali in 2008, at the Museo La Tertulia and Beethoven Concert Hall), Palacios' father, together with fourteen fellow sugar cane reapers, created a sound performance based on the gesture of sharpening their machetes in a sort of *minga* (an indigenous means of organizing collective labor).

Subtly, Palacios' and Castro's works refer to several layers of culturally and historically charged content through sound. Palacios recalls a familial inheritance and tradition passed down from father to son, but also a society that still maintains ways of operating that are based on extractivism and the precarization of labor, bringing to mind the labor of slaves on the colonial hacienda. On the other hand, in an almost anthropological approach, Carlos Castro is interested in cycles, roles, and characters that reemerge throughout history. His work establishes a connection between processes of colonization and expulsion, and between collective and individual dynamics, such as the users of the knives or of the used pipes in the instrument-machines. As Carolyn Birdsall has said, sounds of the past can be constituted as "echoes" in the present, in terms both of interviewee sound memories and of broader cultural narratives concerning social memory and identity. Rather than fix a determined linear narrative or image, sound can be drawn upon to prompt certain moods or feelings (Birdsall, 2009).

Epilogue

On April 28, 2021, an unprecedented social upheaval began in Colombia. The spark for this was a tax reform that sought to impose a tax increase on the middle and lower classes. At night, we heard shots and the intimidating sounds of helicopters, and watched an infinite scroll of videos mentioning the dates, times and places of police outbursts. By day, the street sounded of harangues, newscasts, Molotov cocktails and "less lethal" gunfire in a loop that echoed the complex fabric of Colombian conflicts and triggered social traumas within the population, in what Ben Anderson has called *involuntary remembering*, that enables the past to be re-encountered primarily as a value, unsystematic, [sic] attitude or mood rather than through a representation (2004). I would add that this social trauma is not only triggered in those who directly experienced the war in Colombia, but also in a wider population that has lived the conflict through the media, and through the memories of family and acquaintances.

There is a lot to listen to, here and now. Aural memory is constituted by a complex network of listening perspectives and sonic stimuli such as testimonies, soundscapes (both present and remembered) and every-day sounds, mediated by mass media, or devices such as sound art installations, sound sculptures, and music. Listening is a political act of opening up and reconciling. Still, there is a tension between audio's promise to provide a neutral, just, and objective record, and the interests of whoever is recording and transmitting. Understanding the auditory dimension of conflict and critically listening to the past allows us to become aware of our agency in building the worlds we inhabit. At the same time, it puts into perspective the influence of subjective narrations, mass media, and telecommunications in the narratives we tell, the images and sounds we remember, and the way we construct the present.

References

Akil, Ghofran. *Unresolved.* (Master's thesis, HEAD-Genève, 2019).

Anderson, Ben. 2004. "Recorded music and practices of remembering". Social & Cultural Geography, 5:1: 3-20, https://www.tandfonline.com/doi/full/10.1080/1464936042000181281

Birdsall, Carolyn. 2009. "Earwitnessing: Sound Memories of the Nazi Period". *Sound Souvenirs: Audio Technologies, Memory and Cultural Practices,* edited by Karin Bijsterveld and José van Dijck, 169-181. Amsterdam University Press.

Castillo, Monica, Alen Castaño. 2021. "Lo dulce y amargo del azúcar: el caso de las condiciones laborales de los trabajadores de caña de azúcar de Valle del Cauca (Colombia)". *Boletín de Antropología Universidad de Antioquia* 36 (61): 118-135.

Chaves Castro, Maria Paula. 2014. *Transformaciones de la radio en Colombia: Decretos y leyes sobre la programación y su influencia en la construcción de una cultura de masas.* Monograph, Pontificia Universidad Javeriana.

Gómez Gallego, Jorge Aníbal, José Roberto Herrera Vergara, Nilson. 2010. *Informe final de la Comisión de la Verdad sobre los hechos del Palacio de Justicia.* Bogotá: Editorial Universidad del Rosario.

Kalach Torres, Gina María. 2016. "Las comisiones de la verdad en Colombia." *Revista Jurídica Mario Alario D'Filippo* 8 (16): 106-124.

Martín-Barbero, Jesús. 1993. *Communication, culture and hegemony: From the media to mediations.* London: SAGE Publications Limited.

UN, Human Rights Council. 2021. *Situación de los derechos humanos en Colombia. Informe de la Alta Comisionada de las Naciones Unidas para los Derechos Humanos.* New York: UN Headquarters. https://www.hchr.org.co/index.php/informes-y-documentos/informes-anuales/9562-informe-de-la-alta-comisionada-de-las-naciones-unidas-para-los-derechos-humanos-sobre-la-situacion-de-derechos-humanos-en-colombia-durante-el-ano-2020

Pita Pico, Roger. 2018. "Violencia, censura y medios de comunicación en Colombia: los efectos del Bogotazo y el colapso en las transmisiones radiales." *Revista Anagramas Rumbos y Sentidos de la Comunicación* 17 (33): 153-173.

¿Un arte sonoro menor?: *Dosis de escucha* (2018) y *El aula de los ruidos* (2019)

NORA CASTREJÓN es actriz, productora y gestora cultural. Cursó la Licenciatura en Literatura Dramática y Teatro en la UNAM. Ha colaborado con compañías y creadores de teatro, danza y artes circenses de México, Canadá y Latinoamérica. Fue socia fundadora del Foro Cultural Hilvana en la Ciudad de México. También se ha desempeñado como funcionaria en instituciones culturales públicas y privadas en el área de producción, difusión y programación artística.

FABIÁN AVILA ELIZALDE alias «Neural Xólotl» es artista, docente e investigador independiente en torno a la escucha y las artes sonoras. Estudió la Maestría en Música, Tecnología Musical, y la Licenciatura en Psicología en la UNAM. Es autodidacta en la producción de música electrónica, y se formó en bajo eléctrico y teoría del jazz con Aarón Cruz. Su trabajo artístico y académico ha recibido reconocimientos nacionales e internacionales.

> Quizás las pequeñas historias y las grandes épocas
> nunca son paralelas, los destinos minoritarios son
> escaldados por las políticas de un mercado siempre
> al acecho de cualquier escape.
>
> Y en este mapa ultracontrolado del modernismo
> las fisuras se detectan y se parchan con el mismo
> cemento, con la misma mezcla de cadáveres y
> sueños que yacen bajo los andamios de la pirámide
> neoliberal.
> — Pedro Lemebel

0. Intro

> ¡Felices sean los agrietados, porque ellos dejarán
> pasar la luz!
> — Houria Bouteldja

Para gran parte del gremio artístico, que su obra sea considerada dentro de la esfera de lo *minoritario-menor* es indeseable La construcción de una trayectoria debe apuntar hacia el éxito, el mérito y el reconocimiento, ingresar al «Olimpo de Lxs Consagradxs». Lemebel y Bouteldja son dos potentes invocaciones *minoritarias* para tomar un sendero alejado del pavimento. Consideraremos *lo menor* como una vía para explorar procesos alternativos de escucha y de producción en el arte sonoro, gracias al concepto de *literatura menor* y de la *musiquita*, propuestos por Deleuze y Guattari ([1975] 1990), así como al devenir *minoritario*, cuerpo sin órganos, ritornelo, manada y aparato de captura (Deleuze y Guattari [1980] 2015). Materialzmos tales procesos de escucha en dos obras: *Dosis de escucha* (2018) y

El aula de los ruidos (2019); proyectos fueron apoyados por el *Programa de Estímulo a la Creación y al Desarrollo Artístico CDMX 2017* (PECDA CDMX 2017) y el Instituto Mexicano del Seguro Social (IMSS) respectivamente, así como por el *Programa de Talleres de Artes y Oficios Comunitarios* (TAOC) de la Fábrica de Artes y Oficios Oriente (FARO Oriente).[1]

> [*La musiquita*] comienza por murmurar al oído del que la [escucha] y que se acerca al canto que le envuelve, donde consiente perder su identidad y

---

1 Para todxs esxs niñxs, jóvenes y maestrxs aliadxs con quienes trabajamos años antes: la trabajadora social Carmen Franco en Yuguelito, Iztapalapa; la *Fábrica de ruidos* con *Armstrong Liberado. Colectivo de Música Libre*; Sara Makowski y su manada delirante de *Radio Abierta*; la lucha por la preservación de las lenguas originarias con José Luis Romero en *Arte a 360 Grados*; los intercambios en el *Diplomado Interdisciplinario para la Enseñanza de las Artes en la Educación Básica* (DIPEAEB), coordinado en el Centro Nacional de las Artes por Norma Muñoz y un equipo ampliamente reflexivo; así como los encuentros anti-tanapolítico-eugenésicos de *Comunicarte* con la artista visual y cineasta Sandra Real, la psicóloga Tania Real y su manada de artistas. A todxs esxs cuerpos quisiéramos compartirles:

> En la escuela hay alumnos, no niños. [...] El juego se restringe y hasta las actividades expresivas adquieren una «utilidad». [...] Padres y maestros que promueven la nueva actitud del alumno [...], destacan la importancia de la responsabilidad, el esfuerzo y el estudio. [...] El niño, que en el recreo jugaba libremente con el lenguaje -«uni doli teli catoli, carabín carabí ru ra, ai uan chu merri»-, siente que debe superar rápidamente esa etapa y acomodarse a las nuevas exigencias. [...] Abolir su mirada[-escucha] sensible [...] Todos los niños tienen una mirada poética natural, somos nosotros los que obstruimos su decir haciéndolos vivir en un clima prosaico y hablar en un lenguaje escolar homogéneo y repetitivo. [Sustituyamos] la idea de que es a través del aprendizaje que logramos expresarnos mejor por la idea de que es la necesidad expresiva la que hace posible el aprendizaje. (Calvo 2015)

su lenguaje: Acordaos, un día, antaño, se perdió lo que se [escuchaba]. Acordaos que un día perdisteis *todo* de *todo* cuanto era [escuchado]. Acordaos que es infinitamente triste perder lo que se [escucha]. (Quignard, 2011/ 2019, p. 67)

1. *Bellas Artes* e infantería

Esta mirada retrospectiva es gatillada por el franco desencanto con el arte como práctica, «oficio» y obra derivada en tanto se insiste en su instrumentalización ideológica bajo las nociones de bienestar y progreso. En las operaciones del poder por cooptar el campo de la subjetividad para moldear imaginarios, el arte y lxs artistas hemos sido soldadxs eficientes, incluso sin tenerlo como propósito de origen. Nuestro recorrido comienza por señalar la alianza y sumisión de algunxs artistas al hetero-capitalismo (Silvestri 2020). Lo *minoritario* es paradójicamente acallado cuando pasa por un tamiz artístico que busca visibilizar todo: se pulen los filos a punta de experiencia estética, su potencial de martillo es amortiguado para transformarlo en resanador de astillas y el más brutal de los acontecimientos puede desfilar por la pasarela de la espectacularización. Ese es el costo de «aparecer», de «pasar a la historia», de ser asimilado. A esto, Deleuze y Guattari oponen la fuga, la constante desterritorialización, devenir para no sucumbir: no hay forma de adquirir un cuerpo sin órganos, es necesario hacérselo.

Ya que es a través del cuerpo que se experimenta la vida, decidimos orientar nuestra práctica artística hacia las nociones de juego sensible de manera más bien intuitiva en *Dosis de escucha,* y con más determinación e intención en *El aula de los ruidos*. Este camino nos condujo a cuestionar el lugar del arte sonoro: un campo que se erige disruptivo —porque evidencia los límites expresivos del lenguaje musical y lo abre a yuxtaposiciones inverosímiles con otros territorios artísticos— pero que es conservador en relación a los espacios y actores que le han dado forma y relevancia, en tanto arte fundamentalmente occidental, predominantemente masculino y complaciente con la heterosexualidad como régimen político o, dicho de otra forma, con la ortosexualidad: ORTO-, derecho, recto, estricto, canónico, correctivo como en ortopedia, ortografía, ortodoxia, ortodoncia. Dicha variación sexo-política se erige sobre cuatro pilares: adultismo, sexismo, misoginia y homofobia (Guasch, 2007).

Y así, hay un Arte Sonoro Ortoaural que como estética grita e invita a la heterodoxia e indisciplina, pero cuya praxis es medularmente ortodoxa y elitista. Al menos discursivamente, este propone desterritorializaciones de La Gran Música para contagiarse con otras artes, así como articular lo singular con lo inmediato político, y producir dispositivos colectivos de enunciación; cualidades que resuenan con las características de la *literatura menor*, de acuerdo con Deleuze y Guattari. Sin embargo, ¿acaso este arte sonoro podrá agenciarse un territorio para que surja *la musiquita*, un diminutivo saturado de sonidos desterritorializados, silencios e interrupciones que desarticulen Lo Mayor? ¿Hará de esta prisión que llamamos lenguaje un temblor, un tartamudeo, un estridente silencio que lo granule? ¿Producirá *la musiquita* que con regocijo haga la guerra a la tristeza, al vaciamiento y horror del despliegue orto-tanato-capitalista, a la reterritorialización nociva y a la enunciación autoral individualista? ¿Podrá hacer de la escucha una celebración de lo fúnebre, los desbalances, lxs nunca-escuchadxs, de nuestra homicidad y nuestra estruendosa ternura? Puede ser que la apuesta sea rabiosamente ingenua, pero merece la pena apostar por un arte sonoro *menor-minoritario* que no haga más *musiquita* PARA otros cuerpos, sino CON otros cuerpos, A TRAVÉS de ellos. Hacer de La Gran Música y de El Gran Ruido un ronroneo vibratorio de *soniditos*, *silencitos* y *ruiditos*:

> Los sonidos ya no son solamente sonidos, sino palabras do, re, mi, fa, sol, la, si. Bemoles y sostenidos. Dos de ellos, a una distancia de cuatro o cinco octavas se llaman por el mismo nombre. Si un sonido es tan desafortunado que no tiene un nombre o si parece ser demasiado complejo, lo arrojan fuera del sistema diciendo que es un *ruidito* o un *sonidito* no musical (Cage [1969] 2018).

Aquí resuena que «devenir *minoritario* no es una metáfora» (Silvestri, 2020), sino un cúmulo de flujos para disolver el anhelo de trascendencia: devenir un puñado de *soniditos* inútiles; inutilidad como ocio y regocijo al escuchar una y otra vez los *ruiditos* propios. Interactuemos con *las musiquitas* que puedan producir aquellos cuerpos que El Sistema Mayor expulsa. No más escuchas para vigilarnos, ni las virtuosas ni las activas, sino las nómadas, pasivas, errantes y equivocadas. Añadamos adjetivos a la escucha desde nuestra pequeña singularidad, pues poco importa qué tan modesta sea *nuestra musiquita*, siempre que pueda incomodar al déspota mayor que nos somete.

Proponemos entonces una desarticulación de la elitización del arte sonoro al aproximarlo a poblaciones que este olvida o ignora —salvo cuando las instrumentaliza en un beneficio agregado al mero placer de crear CON otros cuerpos—. En este sentido, ¿cómo puede el arte sonoro nombrar incansablemente a la heterodoxia si sólo produce experiencias para sus públicos y entre sus pares? Ante dicha ortoauralidad —se dirigen solo a poblaciones socioculturamente privilegiadas—, proponemos un resquebrajamiento de tales prácticas.

2. El Gran Ruido y el *ruido menor: la musiquita*

> La música nos protege de los sonidos.
> — Pascal Quignard

Italia, 1913: las orejas como territorio para conmovernos con *El Arte De Los Ruidos*, posterior aliado fascista. Radio Nacional Francesa, 1940: descubren una *musiquita* en las vías del tren e inventan cuatro modos de escucha —ni más, ni menos—. Estados Unidos, 1940: Harry Partch, un *hobo*, *graffitis* como partituras, territorio para vagabundear en cuarenta y tres tonos. John Cage, 1952: 4'33", *TACET*, pieza silenciosa que dinamitó puertas y ventanas de la sala de conciertos para que ingresaran los *ruiditos* expulsados de La Gran Música, para dejar la diminuta belleza desnuda de la duración. Darmstadt, 1958: Sylvano Bussotti con su abierta pasión homoerótica escandaliza a Boulez, mientras que otros rectos compositores le demandaban mesura para no mal influenciar a la juventud (Bogue, 2014). 1961, *Fluxus*: hacer menor a Lo Musical para exaltar lo excluido. Francia, 1968: *Presque Rien No. 1 – Le lever du jour au bord de la mer*, una *casi nada* que arrastró a Luc Ferrari hacia una *musiquita* escondida en amaneceres insomnes a la orilla de una playa, pero que disgustó al *Groupe de Recherches Musicales* (GRM) hasta que lo expulsaron de tan afamado club, pero quien fue cobijado por un Estados Unidos cercano a devenires *minoritarios: free jazz*, minimalismo, tonos senoidales, Marsha Johnson y Sylvia Rivera. Estados Unidos, 1972: despido lésbico de la institución universitaria en las *Sonic Meditations* que instan a reapropiaciones de nuestros sonidos; Pauline Oliveros nos enseña a volar, telepatía, a escuchar los sueños. Invitamos a indagar *Power of Two* (1997-2004), una *musiquita* homoerótica de Barry Truax bajo el formato de ópera electroacústica; a viajar con Wendy Carlos, cuya genialidad al sumergirse en los caprichosos comportamientos del voltaje y la música electrónica fue borrada por los mandatos del hetero-capital; las propuestas psicoacústicas fantasmales de Maryanne Amacher.

¿Y qué ha pasado en México? Disculpen nuestro sesgo al poner por delante La Gran Historia del Ruido, y a la cual pudimos omitir por reiterativa, pero que reinterpretamos para que nuestra sumisión no sea tan evidente. Conocimos algunas *musiquitas* en México gracias a Miguel Molina Alarcón (2015), quien descubrió en el archivo del *Instituto de Investigaciones Estéticas* de la UNAM «un subdesarrollo, un tercer mundo, una *jerga*» (Deleuze y Guattari [1975] 1990, p. 31): un *arte sonoro menor*. Él comenzó su recorrido por las aproximaciones poético-fonéticas de Sor Juana a las vocalizaciones afro e indias en México, para después mostrarnos la *musiquita* de Melesio Morales en su *Sinfonía vapor para banda de música y movimientos y silbatos de locomotora* (1869), con la que exaltaba el nacionalismo del presidente Benito Juárez, afortunadamente estropeada por la lluvia durante su estreno. El *botellófono* que hizo Gran Música para entretener al presidente Porfirio Díaz, pero que ya derramaba flujos desterritorializantes inaudibles para el déspota. José Juan Tablada, un diplomático y poeta, tejedor de un poema sobre ruidos y perfumes. ¿Un «siervo de la nación» que hace *musiquita*? «La contabilidad, la burocracia proceden por calcos; pero también pueden brotar, producir tallos de rizoma, como en una novela de Kafka» (Deleuze y Guattari [1980]2015 20). Otro poeta y «siervo» exclama en su *Comprimido Estridentista* (1921):

> Chopin a la silla eléctrica... Nada de futurismo... Lasso de La Vega... «Estamos lejos del espíritu de la bestia. Como Zaratustra nos hemos librado de la pesadez, nos hemos sacudido los prejuicios. Nuestra gran risa es una gran risa». [...] yo, gloriosamente aislado, me ilumino en la maravillosa incandescencia de mis nervios eléctricos. (Maples Arce 2021)

Una gran carcajada hacia aquél futurismo fascista, un *Comprimido* que incita a electrocutar La Gran Música. Molina nos expuso ante la *musiquita* de las intuiciones ruidistas del burócrata, músico y compositor José Pomar, quien fue un olvidado y un nómada que jamás viajó, pero que en 1922 propuso un *devenir minoritario* al Gran Piano y quien, después, incitado por la duración de la jornada laboral obrera, tituló *Ocho horas* a su ballet ruidista (Muñoz Hénonin, 2016).

Otras obras dignas de mencionar son aquellas del colectivo artístico *No-Grupo*, de quienes recuperamos aquel pequeño concierto de *música plástica*:

> [El] público se interrumpe y se les obsequian unas bolsas de papel estraza. Dentro de cada bolsa hay otra bolsa y dentro de esa bolsa hay otra bolsa, hasta encontrar un papel que dice: «En la experimentación, la diversidad y calidad de los materiales no importan, lo que importa es su trascendencia. RUBÉN VALENCIA Ex artista geométrico lo invita a participar con material de desecho en la exposición que ya fue. Las bolsas que acaba de abrir, son los instrumentos con los que usted mismo ejecutó varios y diferentes sonidos, a través de los cuales se inauguró el primer concierto de música plástica». Después, salen de la sala. (Mirna Castro, comunicación personal, Mayo 21, 2017; Hernández, 2019)

El desecho y lo cotidiano como *musiquita*, lo fútil y lo irrepetible como sonoridades que irrumpieron en el Palacio de Bellas Artes, un lugar supremo para Las Artes Mayores Mexicanas. En este sentido, prestemos oreja a los destellos de *musiquitas* que pasarían desapercibidas si no recordamos la propuesta de Deleuze y Guattari ([1975] 1990) por aproximarnos al *pop* como un posible derrame y fuga de La Gran Música. Hoy celebramos cómo Juan Gabriel, compositor y cantante, precipitó un devenir a dicho palacio;

a veces lo *pop*, como la burocracia en Kafka, decanta flujos *minoritarios*. Un fragmento de la crónica escrita por Carlos Monsiváis ([1990] 2016):

> Uno de los instantes climáticos de sus presentaciones, ocurre durante una canción ranchera, cuando él pregunta «¿Quién se quiere casar conmigo?», y la respuesta es predominantemente o casi exclusivamente masculina. Y los galleros, los alcaldes, los jefes de prensa, los seres temibles a quienes se les atribuye complicidad con las autoridades locales (nueva definición de narcos), los machos bragados, se levantan y aúllan con la sinceridad de quien escenifica la prohibición: «¡Yo, Juanga! ¡Juan Gabriel, eres único! ¡Fíjate en mí! ¡Aquí estoy mírame!», y además de exclamaciones que hace felíz al ejército de psicólogos y psicoanalistas, expertos en el arte de verificar el desbloqueo de los núcleos homosexuales, y quienes por lo demás también gritan para usarse a sí mismos como conejillos de Indias.

Y para cerrar este pequeño viaje por la *musiquita* mexicana, mencionemos a una ruidista que con altísimas intensidades conquistó diversos bloques sonoros, y aun así no figura en La Historia Consagrada: Ruth Aguirre Velasco.

Reiteramos, ¿Es posible un *devenir minoritario* en el arte sonoro? ¿Cómo definirlo?

> [Las minorías se definen] por la distancia que las separa de tal o cual axioma que constituye una mayoría dominante. (Deleuze y Guattari, [1980] 2015 473) [...] Cuanto más se alcanza esta forma de conciencia de minoría, menos solo se siente uno. [...] Uno es una masa en sí mismo por sí solo [...] una

simple potencialidad [...] un elemento para un nuevo devenir. (Deleuze [1972] 2017)

En este sentido, los cuerpos con cáncer y con dolor crónico de una clínica de salud pública, así como lxs niñxs de escuelas en zonas despojadas, tanto para el Gran Arte como para la Gran Academia Objetiva, solo aparecen como materia o sujetos de gran interés, pero jamás como productorxs de obra o de subjetividad. Tales *Grandes,* ante su propia carencia de experiencias vitales transgresoras, se ostentan como elocuentes traductores de las potencias creativas de dichas poblaciones. Por otro lado, cuando lxs niñxs o pacientes de instituciones privadas hacen acciones similares a las que mostraremos, espontáneamente se convierten en Grandes Artistas. Entre más dinero paguen, podrán aspirar a un trato menos carcelario y discriminatorio, en donde todo —muy probablemente— sea cordial, amoroso, integral y dialógico-horizontal. En cambio, en las zonas despojadas, ni siquiera se organiza muestra alguna de las producciones de un taller; si acaso, estas personas serán afortunadxs si no tienen consecuencias por haber faltado a las normas institucionales. Ahora compartimos su *musiquita.*

3. Intercambio de vibraciones:
Dosis de escucha (2018)[2]

> Una canción es una fogata en medio de la tundra.
> — Guadalupe Galván

El valor de *Dosis de escucha* radica en que *lo otro* puede aparecer para apropiarse de eso que se canaliza a través de lo aural. No se banaliza el dolor en pro de su estetización. Es el registro de una vivencia significativa compartida, que también se asumió vulnerable y expuso al fracaso sus propias hipótesis. Esta experiencia surgió del encuentro afortunado con el Dr. José de Jesús Villafaña, director de la Clínica del Dolor y Cuidados Paliativos del Hospital de Oncología del Centro Médico Nacional «Siglo XXI» (IMSS): imaginamos sesiones de escucha en su sala de espera, bajo la inspiración de los protocolos para la escucha organizada de *Ultra-red*, las investigaciones de Mike Nazemi en torno al uso de paisajes sonoros en ambientes clínicos, la *Deep Listening* de Pauline Oliveros y las propuestas de un amplio espectro de artistas sonoros nacionales

---

[2] Invitamos a que acompañen la lectura de esta sección con alguno de los siguientes materiales sonoros, o bien revisen el sitio *web* del proyecto:
- *39:28* por Aarón Cruz: soundcloud.com/user-145619529/3928-2018-aaron-cruz
- *Agosto* por Brian Allen: soundcloud.com/user-145619529/sets/agosto-2018-brian-allen
- *Canto* por Paula Alcázar y Fabián Avila: soundcloud.com/user-145619529/sets/canto-2018-paula-alcazar-fabian-avila
- Sitio web: dosisdeescucha.wordpress.com/

e internacionales. Tejimos una experiencia de poco más de cien sesiones de escucha.

Para el dispositivo médico, el cáncer y el dolor tienden a vaciar las potencias del cuerpo. Nuestro desconocimiento de tales fenómenos nos llevó, primero, a suponer que las personas querrían hablar de sus padecimientos, de los fantasmas que escapan tanto al saber médico como al espiritual, a las aproximaciones psi-, y a todo saber que se erige como benefactor. Pero no querían hablar de eso. Entonces produjimos encuentros dialógicos entre dolor, cáncer y música. Una lucha de espectros con posibilidades de ingresar al cuerpo para transformarlo. No creamos que la música siempre es un encuentro bello.[3]

A la sala de espera llegamos solo con una invitación a la escucha, ya fuera mediante ejercicios inspirados por la *Deep Listening* y *Ultra-red*, o bien por la escucha de música «popular», «experimental-contemporánea» y paisajes sonoros. Preguntamos qué escucharon, qué sintieron, qué imaginaron con los sonido. Y consideramos a sus respuestas *poemitas*, como este:

> Escuché risas y voces, y las olas del mar. Con la música me acordé de mi papá cuando cantaba esas

---

[3] Ver *El odio a la música* (Quignard, 1996/ 2012), y *Música en Auschwitz* (Laks, 1948/ 2018).

canciones. Ahora quisiera ponerle música a mi mamá. [...] Escuché el ruido del agua. Una cascada. Los pájaros. La música. Una canción. Un clavado. [...] El río tranquilo: me dio paz su corriente. Cuando se ponía más fuerte me daba miedo, pero cuando estaba suave, paz. Cuando se puso la canción empecé a dar gracias a Dios porque estamos aquí para hablar de nuestras preocupaciones y nuestro dolor. Me daba estrés porque estoy pendiente por si le hablan a mi esposo. Después me imaginé que cargaba una bolsa con popó, pero después sentí paz, porque Dios está con nosotros. [...] Con la cascada de agua me entró mucho frío. Después me imaginé la compuerta de una presa y me imaginé el metro.

Meses después de realizar el protocolo cada tercer día, nuestro cuerpo ya no quería asistir a la sala. El miedo, la angustia y el dolor eran muy difíciles de transitar, necesitábamos pequeñas alegrías en ese hoyo negro. Nos refugiamos en el psicoanálisis lacaniano, pero ya sabemos qué clase de sacerdocio es hoy. Volvimos para compartir un *remix* extranjero creado en función de aquellos diálogos. Melodías de Bach, Cage, Pärt, Fujieda, Satie: el *Aria* de las *Variaciones Goldberg,* la *Sonata XIII* de las *Sonatas e interludios para piano preparado,* el *Spiegel im Spiegel,* un fragmento del *Pattern of Plants* y la *Gymnopédie No. 1,* respectivamente. Otros *poemitas* surgieron de estas escuchas:

> Tranquilidad. Cambio de lugar. Colores. Del verde al anaranjado. Sueño. Agua relajante. Reflexionar. Cosas positivas. Olvidarnos de algo. Buen volumen.

Pasar con la gente. [...] Cáncer de mama. Aceptarlo.
Piedras que se hacen a un lado. Dios está lejos de
acá, me refiero a lejos de su obra. Cuidar el cuerpo.
[...] Todos vamos a morir. El amor a los hijos. El ogo,
quiero decir ego, nos hace mover los dados. Hay
algo adentro de lo que no tenemos idea clara qué
es [...] Caracol. Ruido de las mariposas. Cascadas.
Viento. Vuelo del águila. *Shepherd Moons* de Enya.
Palo de lluvia. Cuencos. Viola, violín, chelo, piano.
Piano tibetanos. Paisajes mar bosque. Casita con su
chimenea. Pájaros. Espacio desconocido. Llenarse
de vida. Richard Clayderman. Destellos de luz. La
música revive muertos. *Spotify*. Piano de fondo.
Sueño profundo.

Volvimos a la sala junto con una manada de artistas: música y fotografías de Brian Allen; improvisación musical de Aarón Cruz; dibujos, pinturas y ejercicios de dibujo rítmico de Enrique Nájera; documental de *Forastero*; fotografías de Ana Cervantes; diseño gráfico de Mónica Sorroza, junto con sus tarjetas de protección aural y la sugerencia del título final del proyecto; diseño editorial de *Hacklib;* conferencias con Mirna Castro, Rossana Lara, Graciela Martínez, Itze Serrano y Jorge David García —investigadorxs del arte sonoro, la radio y la música—; tutoría artística de Rocío Cerón. Cada quien produjo obras por contactos directos o indirectos con las personas en la sala. Algunas de ellas produjeron poéticas espontáneas: cantar a coro el bolero *Página blanca*; Albina López nos habló sobre cómo transformó a la *Clínica del Dolor* en *Clínica del Amor*; Paula Alcázar

grabó *cancioncitas* «populares» en mensajes de
WhatsApp; compartieron voces, silencios y recuerdos gozosos que aseguraron no volverán. Hubo también quienes hicieron de la música un lugar para dormir, para acariciar a sus acompañantes, sonreír, ponerse ansiosxs o llorar.

Una mañana de agosto, Cruz se arriesgó en una improvisación. De uno se hizo muchxs a través del intercambio de vibraciones: ritornelos desterritorializados que le ayudaron a tejer tranquilidad, bostezos y asombros entre los cuerpos; emergieron sonrisas, descansos y caricias a distancia. Cruz hizo de la sala un poblado para escuchar, un refugio.

Así fue que en estas *Dosis de escucha* apareció *la musiquita* filosófica que Deleuze y Guattari ([1980] 2015) sustrajeron a la terminología musical: el ritornelo; invención continua de cancioncillas para tranquilizarnos, para hacernos un territorio aural durante la espera en la sala que agrietara sus límites en forma de música, diálogos, silencios, acuerdos y desacuerdos que surgieron tras la eclosión singular de cada cuerpo. Además, articuladas en sintonía con las ideas de Virginia Woolf, Leonor Silvestri y Gilles Deleuze en torno a la enfermedad no como un estado de tristeza sino como una potencia, y dado que «una salud frágil mejora la escucha de la vida» (Silvestri, 2021), estas dosis se intensificaron durante aquellos momentos de silencio en los que tejimos un manto audible o quizá aún más durante aquellos momentos en que cesó, gracias a la enfermedad, toda simulación de formalidad:

> En la salud el significado ha usurpado al sonido [...] Pero cuando estamos enfermos, con el policía fuera de servicio, nos arrastramos bajo algún oscuro poema [...] y las palabras emanan su aroma o destilan su esencia, y entonces, si captamos al fin su significado, es mucho más rico por haberlo percibido primero sensualmente, mediante el paladar y las fosas nasales [y las aurales], como alguna fragancia exótica. (Woolf [1925] 2014)

4. Niñxs-monstruxs: *El aula de los ruidos* (2019)

> A las lenguas salvajes no se las puede domesticar, solo se las puede cortar.
> — Gloria Anzaldúa

Flotamos entre los textos pedagógicos de François Delalande, las propuestas no-directivas de Virginia Axline, los rinocerontes en el aula de Murray Schafer, el tomar la palabra mediante la poesía en la escuela de Mercedes Calvo, los flujos creativos de *Fluxus,* Yoko Ono y John Cage, la idea de composición de Jacques Attali, las experiencias artístico-pedagógicas tanto de Jan Rosagel como de Taniel Morales, la pedagogía de la ternura de Lidia Turner y Balbina Pita, las arquitecturas efímeras del juego de Javier Abad, la pedagogía de la escucha de Carla Rinaldi, las reflexiones sobre el disciplinamiento escolar del cuerpo en Michel Foucault, y el hacerse un cuerpo sin órganos y el ritornelo de Deleuze y Guattari.

El programa comunitario-pedagógico tradicional de la FARO Oriente nos brindó la oportunidad de experimentar procesos antiautoritarios de educación artística en escuelas públicas de educación básica, a pesar de no contar con presupuesto alguno. Tal condiciónnos llevó a estimular una escucha artísticamente orientada mediante el uso de materiales cotidianos para provocar experiencias sonoras efímeras: improvisaciones e instalaciones con el mobiliario y utensilios disponibles en el salón de clases —butacas, cuadernos, lápices, pizarrones, entre otros—, así como caminatas sonoras en el patio escolar.[4]

Así, esta obra desmonta y confronta la propia configuración disciplinaria y normativa de la escuela que se impone aún en prácticas que suponen el ejercicio de la creación en libertad. Seamos honestxs: un salón de clases de una escuela pública de una zona «marginal» poco tiene que ver con un museo o con

---

4 Les invitamos a mirar un breve vídeo retrospectivo de la experiencia: <u>youtu.be/UhwNvWhf-CM</u>

una idílica comunidad Waldorf o Montessori. Un niño que tiene dentro de su lista de sonidos favoritos las detonaciones de un arma de fuego, no es la clásica representación de la imaginación infantil. En estos espacios, la manipulación de unx artista para «enseñar a escuchar» sin despojarse de sus propios prejuicios de «lo estético», habría resultado en una frustración estéril.

Durante todo el proceso, apelamos a la inteligencia e intuición de lxs niñxs, y procuramos tener una disposición para apreciar en el caos y la destrucción, la presencia de flujos creativos inesperados de imaginación, ternura y alegría. Pusimos a su servicio recursos materiales para producir una experiencia estético-afectiva singular: que una niña pueda, literalmente, bañarse de color púrpura hasta vivenciar en su cuerpo la intensidad de dicho tono y su regocijo al apropiárselo en una pequeña acción. Escuchar sonidos insólitos en los troncos de los árboles del patio ante la presencia incrédula de la maestra, quien impedida para escuchar los pasos de las hormigas o un bosque lleno de bestias, exigía que le diéramos respuesta acerca de si acaso lxs niñxs mentían o alucinaban. Todo esto tal vez equivalga a incumplir La Misión-Visión-Meta-Estrategia-Intervención que se pretende durante el «taller de artes». Expulsemos de nuestra subjetividad semejante instrumentalización:

> Cuanto más se hace practicar la tonalidad y cuanto más inteligente y eficazmente se lo hace [...], mayores son las dificultades de los niños luego para escuchar músicas extra-europeas y músicas contemporáneas. [...] El resultado es una reacción de rechazo [y] su respuesta es siempre la misma: «Eso no es música». (Delalande [1984] 1995)

A mayor estratificación de la escucha, menor posibilidad de devenir *minoritaria* para hacer *nuestra musiquita*. Los cuerpos de «lxs menores de edad» son continuamente violentadxs por el sistema educativo ortodoxo al inocularles disciplina y vigilancia para ahuyentar cualquier variación creativa que se desvíe de los resultados esperados. Por ello pensamos formas cautelosas que despertaran sus potencias aurales y de experimentación sensorial, para propiciar un acercamiento a la fábrica interior de estxs niñxs. Por ejemplo, no dañarse a sí mismxs, ni a sus compañerxs, así como la disposición para aceptar incondicional y positivamente sus propuestas imaginativas y artísticas. Es necesario compartir bloques de aquellos breves tejidos:

> Dos niñas se preguntaban entre sí: «¿Cuál es el sonido de las alas de una mariposa?»/ Al dibujar animales y la forma en que imaginaban sus sonidos, un niño dijo: «Este caballo hace todos los sonidos que hacen todos los caballos, pero le dibujé este globito con notas musicales, porque todas las noches

sueña con cantar.»/ Fabricaron instrumentos de ruido con un par de abatelenguas y un trozo de papel al centro; dedujeron el intercambio vibratorio entre sus cuerpos, el papel y la madera. Lo que escucharon: caballos galopando, graznidos de patitos, trompetas, millones de elefantes, tránsito vehicular, un lenguaje para mensajes secretos, aullidos, una manada de delfines./ En el reverso de uno de sus mapas, después de una caminata sonora y de preguntarles qué escucharon, se leía: «El viento y es ermoso.» [sí, sin hache, para librarnos de la prisión de La Lengua Mayor]. El mapa pertenecía a un equipo formado solo por niños, y en el que todos y cada uno negaron la escritura de la frase, e insistieron en culpar a las niñas de haber saboteado su mapa: siempre recordaremos el rostro de aquel niño en el patio, lleno de ternura, indescriptible, y quien con los ojos cerrados escuchaba al viento, lleno de asombro.

Compartimos las tardes durante cuatro meses, y después tuvimos que decir: «Adiós, me voy, y en mi corazón llevaré...» (Deleuze y Parnet [1996] 2021). En nuestra exploración final de territorios creamos pequeñas melodías ruidosas, *musiquitas* que nos dieran el valor para volver a nuestras casas durante la noche. Quizá se nos podría advertir que romantizamos la niñez, pero nada más lejos. Durante nuestros encuentros, una manada no cesó de crear una composición ruidista en el aula mediante el choque veloz de las sillas, y cuyo público fue nuestra escucha, y el rostro desconcertado de la maestra, quien después nos preguntó cuál era el objetivo; no se le juzgue, pues sus preguntas reflejaban un

interés sincero por saber. Cuando una niña fugada
de la prisión del lenguaje y «los buenos modales»
pero catalogada por el ejército psi- como «deficien-
te-retrasada» mezcló los gestos que acordamos colectiva y previamente para crear una improvisación
llena de contrastes y matices, de tal *bellecita*, que
dejó atónitxs a sus compañerxs y al maestro. Otra
niña, al darse cuenta sobre cómo la falda limitaba su
improvisación, creó un modo para brincar sobre las
sillas y mesas porque no aceptaba que solo los niños
lo hicieran; las demás la siguieron para componer un
delirio percutivo. Y es que lxs niñxs —al igual que lxs
poetas— usan dos acepciones de la palabra «creo»:
dar por cierto algo que no está comprobado y producir algo de la nada; y «nadie puede restringir su libertad para inventar una realidad a su antojo [pues]
todo forma parte de un universo donde no existen los
límites y donde nada es imposible» (Calvo, 2015).

Por eso hoy recordamos también a aquellxs ni-
ñxs-máquinas-de-guerra de la Alcaldía Iztacalco,
quienes para contar una historia de terror repre-
sentaron con globos una masacre militar en la que
los globos pequeños no podían morir hasta que,
de súbito, todos resucitaron, incluso lxs militares
asesinos; a la niña que nos contó sobre un unicornio
semejante a una gran bestia-dinosaurio devoradora

de las cosas que no le gustaban de sus cuidadorxs; los dibujos de banderas mexicanas que se derretían para originar animales. Está de más interpretar esta *musiquita* como metáforas edípico-familiares, pensamientos irracionales o sueños producidos por la televisión y los videojuegos, pues son más bien un ruidoso pronunciamiento.

Si se asume que la conciencia propicia *mayuscularse* así como eliminar a *lo minusculado* (Deligny [1995] 2021), entonces invitemos a la educación artística, las arte-terapias y demás exploraciones burocráticas del arte como re-sanador del tejido social a *minuscularse* en una fábrica amoral de intensidades no para hacer-el-bien-por-lxs-niñxs: «el bien vehiculiza las peores catástrofes» (Silvestri 2020). A cambio, hagamos un espacio para atizar la pira que acabe por extinguir un edificio del que ya solo quedan ruinas. Que emerjan de los escombros lxs niñxs-monstruxs, en el sentido etimológico que refiere a lo prodigioso y sobrenatural, a quienes muestran el futuro —y el pasado y el presente—, y que nos advierten la voluntad de lxs diosxs:

> Si no fuese porque me resigno a un mundo que me obliga a ser sensata, gritaría de susto ante las alegres monstruosidades de la tierra. Solo un infante no se espanta: también él es una alegre monstruosidad que se repite desde el comienzo de la historia del hombre. (Lispector [1978] 1999)

5. O(u)tro

> ¿Es el sonido lo que desaparece, o soy yo?
> — Pauline Oliveros

Hemos dicho que los procesos artísticos han de alejarse de los aparatos de captura, pues de otro modo terminarían siendo un ejército que bloquea los flujos vitales de las comunidades para imponerles aquellos que les conecten al deseo despótico: las comunidades son quienes les regalan la voz que hace falta al arte, no a la inversa. También expusimos una breve historia de *las musiquitas* mexicanas con la finalidad de subrayar inicios anteriores a los procesos europeos «vanguardistas», solo que teñidos por otros brotes y agenciamientos. En cada una de las obras compartidas no hablamos en nombre de las personas sino que expusimos sus palabras y sonidos: no hay algo más grosero y narcisista —Talón de Aquiles de El Gran Arte— que hacer decir a otrxs lo que unx quisiera decir. Nos alejamos del canto repetitivo en torno al sedimento institucional para, como Kafka, propiciar el brote de algunas pequeñas hierbas menos endurecidas. Estos procesos no son en sí replicables, pero tienen la posibilidad de conectarse a lo que mejor convenga a quienes nos han acompañado hasta aquí: «Hay que detener la repetición, transformar el mundo en forma de arte y la vida en un inestable disfrute» (Attali [1977] 2011).

Un pequeño arte que vuelva a encantar al mundo y la escucha, pero no permanezcamos impávidxs ante la peligrosa idealización de la segunda —de nuevo Platón y sus espectros—. En cambio, iniciemos una pesquisa de sus potencias nocivas para aprender, como en *Hamlet,* a escurrir un veneno en las orejas de lxs reyes y su corte de cretinxs, o a conocer los mecanismos mediante los que ellxs desarticulan a los cuerpos; la ortoauralidad es un despliegue disciplinador que ojalá se derrumbe. *Remix* a Pauline Oliveros: ¿Serán los sonidos de aquellxs reyes y sus fieles cretinxs lo que desapareceremos, o serán estos quienes nos desaparezcan?

Referencias

Attali, Jacques. 2011. *Ruidos. Ensayo sobre la economía política de la música*. Traducido por Ana María Palos. Ciudad de México: Siglo XXI.

Bogue, Ronald. «Scoring the Rhizome: Bussotti's Musical Diagram». *Deleuze Studies* 8, N° 4 (2014): 470-490.

Cage, John. 2018. *Del lunes en un año*. Traducido por Isabel Fraire. Ciudad de México: Alias.

Calvo, Mercedes. 2015. *Tomar la palabra. La poesía en la escuela*. Ciudad de México: Fondo de Cultura Económica.

Delalande, Francois. 1995. *La música es un juego de niños*. Traducido por Susana G. Artal,). Buenos Aires: Melos Ricordi Americana.

Deleuze, Gilles. 2017. *Derrames. Entre el capitalismo y la esquizofrenia*. Traducido por Equipo Editorial Cactus). Buenos Aires: Cactus.

Deleuze, Gilles y Guattari, Félix. 1990. *Kafka. Por una literatura menor*. Traducido por Jorge Aguilar Mora. Ciudad de México: Era.

Deleuze, Gilles y Guattari, Félix. 2015. *Mil mesetas: Capitalismo y esquizofrenia*. Traducido por José Vázquez Pérez y Umbelina Larraceleta . Madrid: Pre-Textos.

Deligny, Fernand. 2021. *Cartas a un trabajador social*. Traducido por Sebastián Puente. Buenos Aires: Cactus.

Guasch, Ò. 2007. *La crisis de la heterosexualidad*. Barcelona: Laertes.

Hernández, Rolando. «Nosotros desmaterializamos. Conceptualismo y prácticas colectivas en torno al sonido durante la década del 70 en Latinoamérica». *Medium*, Noviembre 18, 2019. https://medium.com/@lanoisyone/nosotros-desmaterializa-mos-d09105f93e88

Lispector, Clarice. 1999. *Un soplo de vida (Pulsaciones)*. Traducido por Mario Merlino. Madrid: Siruela.

Maples Arce, Manuel. «Actual No. 1: Hoja de Vanguardia. Comprimido Estridentista». International Documents of Latin American and Latino Art, Museum of Fine Arts, Houston, Septiembre 16, 2021. https://icaa.mfah.org/s/es/item/737463

Molina Alarcón, Miguel. (2015). «Arte Sonoro en JustMAD. Miguel Molina Alarcón». EX Asociación de arte electrónico y Experimental, Septiembre 18, 2021. https://arteelectronico.net/arte-sonoro-en-justmad-miguel-molina-alarcon/

Monsiváis, Carlos. «Juan Gabriel y aquel apoteósico y polémico concierto en Bellas Artes». *Proceso*, Agosto 29, 2016, https://www.proceso.com.mx/cronica/2016/8/29/juan-gabriel-aquel-apoteosico-polemico-concierto-en-bellas-artes-169702.html

Muñoz Hénonin, Maby. 2016. «José Pomar y su música para piano: Una aproximación a la obra y al compositor»: Tesis de Maestría, Universidad Nacional Autónoma de México.

Quignard, Pascal. 2019. *Butes.* Traducido por Miguel Morey y Carmen Pardo. Madrid: Sexto Piso.

Silvestri, Leonor. «1000 mesetas. Leonor Silvestri» Octubre 20, 2020. Lista de videos,. https://youtu.be/MpEZ-2ky9HM

Silvestri, Leonor. «Nietzsche Soberbia. Estados valetudinarios. Leonor Silvestri». Abril 16, 2021. Video, 1:18:32. https://youtu.be/20XKjcErWs0

Woolf, Virginia. (2014). *De la enfermedad.* Traducido por Ángela Pérez. Barcelona: José J. de Oñaleta Editor.

Indigenous and Anticapitalist Sounds: Musical Practices to Pollinate the Brazilian Caatinga

ALEXANDRE HERBETTA is an associate professor of Social Anthropology and works at the Takinahaky Center for Indigenous Higher Education and the Postgraduate Studies in Social Anthropology of the Federal University of Goiás (UFG). A researcher at the Center for Decolonial Practices and Knowledge/NTFSI and IMPEJ – Center for Indigenous Ethnology/PPGAS/UFG, Herbetta has experience in anthropology, politics and education, with emphasis on decoloniality, participatory methodologies, interculturality and indigenous ethnology.

PAULO ANTONIO KALANKÓ has been the political leader and chief of the Kalankó people for more than 30 years and is a recognized indigenous political leader in the region. Antonio Kalankó is also a master of indigenous musicality, and is a great connoisseur of the musical ritual of *Toré*.

Fig. 1. The Praiá Dancer, who represents a spiritual entity important to the traditional musical ritual system. The entity is also important to community decision making (and is a repository of great environmental knowledge).

Listen:

Audio 1. Toré Music:
Subi-no-alto-do-tempo

From the sound landscape of the Alagoas Caatinga, in northeastern Brazil, several types of sounds emerge. Some, such as the roaring of cattle, are a feature of rural areas while others are typically urban, such as the gathering of children returning from school, the combination pointing to the complexity of the place, urban life intertwined with a rural environment. Likewise, the area is characterized by the expansion of agricultural activities on small and medium farms, and by the small and middle-sized cities that have developed over the last decades, the result of an unbalanced urbanization process, guided by the mechanisms of coloniality.

In this landscape of sound, it is important to mention the profusion of sounds from the birds and creatures that populate and pollinate the biome beautifully, besides generating life. There is a close relationship between these sounds and the different species of flowers that color the environment, and the fruits that promote well-being and health, such as the umbu fruit. The combination of these sounds and relationships forms a soundscape, as Schafer (2001 [1977]), who understands this as a sound environment, explains.

The Caatinga and all its profusion of sounds, relationships, knowledge and species is one of the most threatened regions on the planet. It has suffered an intense process of desertification, which substantially affects the lives of the people, their knowledge, and the species that live there. In addition, this process affects not only the possibilities, but also the life-giving potential of the region. Several indigenous peoples still make their living space within this biome, which is, therefore, a place of pluri-epistemologies and diverse ontologies, rather than a place intended only for the production of goods.

In the soundscape of this region, especially in the indigenous territories, the unique sound of indigenous music stands out, the vibrating and powerful sound of the *Toré* a true epistemological and ontological matrix for "good living (*bem viver*)", a balanced and healthy indigenous way of being-in-the-world typical of South American indigenous peoples.

The musical ritual of Toré was often harshly repressed by local elites, as part of a constant epistemic violence. Although once seen as merely a cultural performance, diacritically marking out the indigenous identity, Toré is much more than that!

A polysemic musical ritual with political and epistemic anti-capitalist values, Toré has the potential to decolonize the caatinga. The practice of Toré is outlined as the way in which indigenous peoples reflect, maintain and produce new ways of knowing and being-in-the-world. The practice is furthermore based on other categories and notions of allowing other life possibilities.

Our mother tongue resides in our music; it is a document that keeps us alive in the territory. It keeps us going. It is maintenance! It makes us stronger! It is a cure. We feel it on our skin.

The relationship betweenbirds, flowers and plants leads to a lively and diverse Caatinga. In the process another soundscape based on a variety of other sounds, human and non-human, emerges as the "enchanted" ones, vital entities of indigenous spirituality. This takes place in relation to nature, perceived from an indigenous point of view, rather than through the Cartesian dichotomy, based on Western ontology, that separates nature from culture.

Accordingly, in Toré the Caatinga is musicalized and pollinated, and remains alive. Our aim is to present part of the cosmopolitical aspect in the sound of the Toré songs, based on an idea of the "living Caatinga" that opposes the current desertification process of the biome. The "living Caatinga" is the driving force behind the decolonization of space and for the practice of anti-capitalist resistance, and calls attention to new relationships and possibilities.

The idea of interconnectedness is vital to the living Caatinga. Therefore, we look forward to presenting the Toré as the assumption of another caatinga, not degraded, not turned into a desert, but full of life, and pollinated!

Fig. 2. Spiritual leader guiding Praiá dancers in a musical ritual called the Praiá Ritual, which is part of the musical ritual system for which Toré is the basis.

Territory

The Kalankó, an indigenous population, consists of about 400 people who live in the interior of northeastern Brazil, in the high hinterlands of Alagoas, specifically in the municipality of Água Branca. Even today, the community still does not have a demarcated indigenous land. This process has been dragging on for years at the National Indigenous Foundation (FUNAI), the state institution responsible for indigenous issues. The demarcation would guarantee not only the physical and cultural maintenance of the group, but also the conservation of the Caatinga.

The Kalankó territory, fragmented into small landholdings, and small and medium-sized properties belonging to indigenous and non-indigenous people, is increasingly affected by non-indigenous production activities and land expropriation. Some predatory activities practiced by the non-Indigenous are easily identified in this territory, including fruit production; the grazing of a small herd of cattle and goats; a transporter company; ostrich production; wood for charcoal and stakes, among other activities. In addition, there is the advance of the non-indigenous landowners who end up appropriating more land year by year, pressuring the indigenous population into ever-smaller portions of land, with fewer necessities for survival.

This process of territorial expropriation and ecological degradation is responsible for the scarcity of the resources that are vital for the life of the indigenous population. Jardilina Kalankó says that "we plant watermelon, but when summer comes, everything dries up". For the Kalankó shaman Tonho Preto "the cotton crop has been reduced by more than half, the cotton is extinct. It doesn't rain in the summer anymore". Likewise, "the *caroá* is being lost. It is part of religion. One vestment needs 150 dozen kilos of caroá, which is scarce. Today there are 12 Praiá vestments, made with great difficulty, besides being scarce, we are supplying other people, too".

The caroá is a type of bromeliad typical of the Caatinga. From the fiber of its leaves, important objects are made by the indigenous population of the region, such as the Praiá garment for dancers. The Praiá dancer (fig. 1) represents the enchanted entities that are the basis of the indigenous spiritual world. Such a situation underlines the relationality that is fundamental to the Kalankó epistemology: without territory, there is no caroá, greatly affecting the spiritual practice of the collective.

The Kalankó live in degraded parts of the Brazilian Caatinga, one of the regions in Brazil that is most threatened and transformed by anthropic action (Souza, 2004, pp. 4-8). The Caatinga houses a typical Brazilian biome, with low rainfall and high average temperatures throughout the year. It has high biodiversity and covers about 700 thousand km² of the nation's territory. Currently, about 80% of its area is affected by anthropic changes. This is typical of Brazilian predatory capitalism, threatening a dramatic scenario for the nation's future sustainability. The Caatinga is dying. It is inarguable that Brazilian governments have always collaborated with the degradation of the biome. Only 5% of the Caatinga is a preservation area and less than 1% is indigenous land. Notably, the deforestation rate in the country is increasingly high, at a time when there is a far-right government ruling the country.

We want the land in order to preserve natural resources, traditional medicine, forests, streams. The hinterlands need to be cultivated. Besides, the land sustains natural resources, medicine, springs, forests, streams, music and life. The land needs to be cultivated and planted with corn, cassava, cotton and watermelon. The spirituality of the indigenous people is to guard the land to preserve its natural resources, and to use the soil to cultivate and produce food, to guarantee well-being.

The Toré

The Toré is part of a musical-ritual system that also includes the Praiá and the Service de Chão. This musical genre extends across a large part of the interior of Alagoas and beyond. In each Toré ritual, at least three songs must always be sung, producing an enchanted energy that comes from the presence and action of the enchanted entities in the ritual arena – the *"terreiro"*. According to Culezinha Kalankó, the "terreiro" "is meant to receive this energy that is responsible for health, safety, and joy".

Zé Kalankó states that he "was born in the Toré," and will die in it. To Tonho Kalankó, "Toré is the music

Fig. 3. A great Toré circle. A good example of a Toré practice in the middle of Caatinga in Kalankó territory.

Listen:
Audio 2. Toré Music: Feathered Caboclo

that has always been sung", since their ancestors. As for Maria Kalankó, "one cannot live without Toré." Often, it seems as if Toré is the basis for the formation of subjectivities. To be born in the Toré means discovering oneself as a subject alongside authorizing, recognizing and appropriating to oneself a way of existing in this world.

Furthermore, it is in the domain of the Toré that one catches sight of a series of practices, notions, ideas, and feelings that can be appreciated in relation to life, where one connects the body to a way of being. To illustrate this point, in the Toré one always seeks to dance in pairs; this brings about the logic of association, in the case of bodies, entities that should not isolate themselves. The dance is based on the "core-periphery" structure, in which the singers stand in the center of the circle and the other participants on the margins. The dance is always performed counterclockwise, and the moves consist of twirls and turns.

The singing is based on a "question-answer" structure, in which the singer sings two verses, and the participants answer with two more, as well as some variations of this basis. All Kalankó musical pieces are reiterative in the sense that they take on a new meaning and resume a path already demonstrated by the group. The more the dynamic is repeated, the more enchanted energy is produced in the moment. Toré is reiterative also because it happens through the repetition of certainsound figures – melodic cells, similar rhythms, relations and elements proper to the epistemology in focus. The music also reiterates certain terms, which can be characters, objects, or actions proper to the environment.

Kalankó musicality is about the Caatinga. There are many melodic procedures, demonstrating that the Toré is based on creativity and freedom. The melodic phrase is composed of two parts, evenly shared, always ending at the bottom. Also notable aresome procedures within the melodic composition, such as the profusion of arpeggios, ornamentation, rhythmic moves between singer and chorus, and also between men and women, interpolation and stacking.

Fig. 4. Toré Musical Transcription which points to musical and epistemological elements based on Caatinga indigenous perception.

Even though the Toré is called a *"promessa"* or *"brincadeira"*, "it is about respect," as Mr. Edmilson, a great Toré master says, due to its importance in producing social relations and lifestyles, and its connection to territory. The rite can be performed in several spaces, from inside an individual's home, to outside a village's bounds. Toré is usually performed in the farmyard, a rectangular space located in the center of a village. When such rites also assume an external political significance, they demonstrate a diacritical sign of ethnic identification.

Urubu de Serra Negra
    Urubu de Serra Negra
    de velho caiu as penas (Cantador)
    de come mangaba verde
    na baixa da jurema. (Cantador)
    Ole le coã (Coro)
    na baixa de jurema
    olele coã
    na baixa da jurema ole le coã

Serra Negra Vulture
    Serra Negra Vulture
    so old its legs fell off (Singer)
    from eating green mangaba
    in the lowlands of the jurema. (Singer)
    Ole le coã (Audience response)
    in the low jurema
    ole le coã
    in low jurema ole le coã

Fig. 5: Aunt Maria Kalankó, who represents one of the first generations to inhabit this part of the Brazilian Caatinga following the violent forced movement suffered by indigenous Pankararu in Pernambuco state.

Listen:
Audio 3. Toré Music: Serra Negra Vulture

Associations and relations: Flowers, birds, fruit and territory

Each song in the Kalankó village belongs to an enchanted entity, the musical 'owner' of the work. In this case, the owner of the Toré "Serra Negra Vulture", above, is from Andorinha master, which points to a bird from the region. Analysis makes it clear that the main relationship in the song is between sky and earth. In it, the vulture, another bird, represents the higher ground, since it is a bird that flies high.

The vulture that comes from above has eaten green *mangaba*, a regional fruit. The act of eating here implies a transformation, which results in the feathers falling out, diminishing the power of the animal. The *jurema*, a vegetable, is located in a region classified as lowland. The term jurema, in geography, identifies something similar to a low altitude valley. The jurema is placed in opposition to the mangaba, a much-appreciated fruit, that seems to be in an intermediate realm, neither low on the ground nor set on high. The sensitive code that becomes evident is taste. Such relations are often present in the songs.

More than that, the Kalankó people have an amazing knowledge of the plant and animal species of the Caatinga. This knowledge is put into use in healing procedures, cooking, territorial management, and in ritual musical moments. Part of this knowledge refers to the understanding and classification of a number of birds, such as *Gavião Caburé* (barred forest falcon), *Viuvinha* (barn swallow), *Andorinha* (swallow), *Acoã* (laughing falcon), *Urubu* (vulture) and others. When they appear in the Toré, the birds of the Caatinga usually represent the enchanted entities that, while still alive, have transcended into the spiritual world and protect the community.

In relation to what has been said, the Kalankó, while referring to themselves – subjects – identify themselves as standing on the lower ground, therefore distant from the birds that occupy the higher level. Accordingly, they elaborate a series of correlations with the plant order, that is to say, the vegetal world. Flowers, in Toré music, for example, are taken as subjects of the group. The narrative itself is created to locate the group in the indigenous universe of the region, based, for example, on metaphors of a phylogenetic kind, which involves, on one side, the "Old Trunks", that represent the ancestors, and, on the other side, the "Rama Tips", the "new" communities.

It can be said that the Kalankó (a farming population)'s cosmovision, has two base layers, the high and the low, represented by the sky and the earth. In this scenario, the indigenous person must work towards the conjunction of both in order to promote contact with the enchanted world, which can give access to the vital energy – the enchanted one – that manifests abundantly in non-degraded places. This conjunction has to do with the action of singing. To make it happen, sound is used as an agent of the conjunction. Kalankó musicality establishes a complex network of relations between species that articulates the sky with the earth, the birds with the flowers, and the Toré with the territory.

Territorial Songs

The Toré songs are territorial, as Julio Kamer Apinajé states, speaking of Panhi musicality. For Kamer Apinajé (author), it is necessary to sing the traditional songs to ensure the sustainability of both the population and the world. Territory, therefore, is not only a space of intensified commodity production. On the contrary, territory is intrinsically connected with other areas of life, such as social organization, ritual, access to natural resources, health, musicality, and, finally, indigenous existence itself (Kamer and Herbetta, 2018).

According to Floriberto Diaz Gomes, a Mixe intellectual:

> It is not madness or superstition that our fathers and mothers taught us that we should talk to the earth to cultivate it, or that trees, birds, and rivers are our brothers, and that we should do rituals and life ceremonies at least once a year, to look at ourselves and realize that our life is the smallest point in the cosmos, but perhaps one of the most important in creation (Hernandez and Jimenez, 2014, p. 49).

Toré, then, proposes a living Caatinga effectively based on relations and principles, with an axis of other classifications and distinct relations between species and territory, for instance, among territory, bromeliads, birds, plants, other animals, healing, the body, and the spiritual world. To take into consideration this other way of perceiving and producing the Caatinga is to decolonize its current management. Singing the Toré is a proposal of transformation.

In opposition, the destruction of part of the territory to generate capital for a few individuals is evident. This implies destroying not only the territory, but all of the spiritual and ancestral knowledge that is learned from/with nature, and disrupting a series of ancestrally established relationships.

Listen:
Audio 4. Toré Music: Aldeia tem caboclo

<u>Pollination as a deep connection</u>

The text presented here is the result of a long and intense dialogue between a great Toré master, Chief Paulo Kalankó, and researcher Alexandre Herbetta. We have tried to present, from our own memories and knowledge, remarkable features and affective elements of the musical tradition, based on our distinct points of view. At some points the pronoun "we" is used, indicating the possibility of an intercultural collective, something that is vital to the contemporary world. In others, individual songs, sounds and memories are the gateway to good and proper communication.

We have tried to highlight how the practice of musical ritual is the concrete epistemic and ontological proposition of another way of being and, consequently, of another handling of the world. The concept of Kalankó music, for example, is distinct from that of music in the Eurocentric Western world. The concept of development is the same. According to Oyeronké Oyewumi, "societies that have experienced colonization have suffered many negative effects, some psychological, some linguistic, and some intellectual. However, perhaps none has been less studied than how colonization subjugates knowledge and marginalizes local epistemes" (2016, p. 1).

Sousa Santos (2007, p. 14) asserts that "the understanding of the world far exceeds the Western understanding of the world". In brief, the musical structure evidenced in Kalankó music reveals a world in which the enchanted spiritual entity (and its energy) is seen in and relates to birds, whether the hawk, the acauã, the parrot or another bird species, while the

Indigenous people that interacts with these birds, relates to the plant world, often refering to types of flower. The intermediate world is constituted of elements located in the middle of the other two layers, such as fruits—mangaba, murici and umbu—and are affected by taste, which leads to transformation.

The Toré musical tradition, therefore, establishes connections and effects the varied relationships between the elements mentioned above, as well as others that did not appear in the Toré discussed here, in the process demonstrating a grammar of decoloniality (Mignolo, 2010). Associations between species creates life in the Caatinga, as does access to an enchanted energy that is responsible for the health and happiness of the people.

This process is somewhat similar to pollination. The relationship between birds and flowers generates the abundance and multiplicity of species—the living caatinga!

Such a proposition reaffirms what Shawn Wilson, an intellectual of Cree Indigenous roots postulates about indigenous way of thinking. For Wilson, the relationality of the indigenous peoples is central to their distinct organizations and behaviors. It is notable that, from an indigenous perspective, the universe is not understood in a fragmented manner, based on Western dichotomies of nature and culture, body and mind, reason and emotion.

For Arturo Escobar, it is possible to think of this dynamic – as well as similar dynamics – from the perspective of relational ontology. According to the author (Escobar, 2016, p. 113), [...] relational ontologies are realized in cultivation practices similar to traditional peasant husbandry (polyculture with production for subsistence and for the market, a diversified landscape with links to communities and gods, etc.). In the same vein, Mignolo and Tlostanova (2012, p. 232) suggest that the most appropriate term for this type of situation is "vincularidad," reflecting a deep inter-connectivity that deals with the relationships among the various elements, as well as the constant correlations between them. The relationship can feed back into the system, giving a more complex aspect to the various networks of association so established.

Moreover, the elements identified in analysing the Toré songs are multiple and interrelated, expressing arrangements that connect the Caatinga, the animal and floral species, the humans, the songs, and the spiritual entities. This indicates a specific notion of territory, i.e., that the enchanted ones, the birds, other animals, fruits, movements, objects, and people exist only to the extent that they are associated.

Humans and non-humans, different species, can therefore coexist in a respectful and balanced way that breaks with western dichotomies. Important elements, but fragmented and isolated from the complexity of life when it is reduced to the notion of predatory exploitation, such as development, backwardness, income generation, employment, and market economics, all typical of a westernized matrix of knowledge, should not play a central role in the management of the territory in question.

While the Caatinga of Alagoas – and Brazil in general – continues to be exploited in a destructive way that isbased on a developmental and predatory capitalism, undergoing an intense process of desertification, as we have seen, the Kalankó continue to have the biome as a space for survival, a place for the production of a universe of life and well-being – not only for the production of commodities.

Broadly speaking, the end of the Caatinga is the end of the enchanted birds and indigenous flowers, and of the relationships between the species. The Toré is then more than a diacritical marker that points to an indigenous belonging. The Toré is the proposition of another Caatinga—not degraded, not turned into a desert, but full of life. A musical territory and a pollinated one.

To this extent, Immanuel Wallerstein notes the importance of the present moment in the unfolding of the contemporary world. He claims that the modern world system is currently facing a fundamental bifurcation; "it is going through a systemic crisis that also affects the structures of knowledge. We have before us not one, but two great social uncertainties: what will the nature of the new historical system we are building be, and what will the epistemology of our new structures and knowledge be" (Wallerstein, 2004, p. 48).

We fight for a music-filled, alive, pollinated Caatinga. For an interconnected Caatinga, too. We plead the importance of the assumption of pluri-epistemologies. We believe that interculturality can be fundamental to the elaboration of public policies that effectively seek sustainability. Similarly, we fight for the Toré. Our fight is to demarcate the Kalankó land. Once our own land is secured, our lives will get better. It is our right. We are both indigenous and citizens.

I will never forget a Toré that took place on the final night of the "Meeting of the Indigenous Peoples of the Northeastern Hinterlands", in 2007. Throughout the day, joy was evident in the Toré circles, where the laughter and joy were visible on everyface. At the same time, suffering was an ever-present theme in the speeches of the leadership, focusing on the struggle of the indigenous peoples to have their rights respected within the country, asking for respect from the Federal Government.

It was very cold in the Caatinga that night and it started to rain, preventing the anticipated Praiá Rite from taking place. I heardresigned comments saying that this is just how an Indigenous life is – difficult. The constantly-lit bonfire was almost extinguished by of the rain as it began to fall heavily, also threatening the final Toré. This Toré would gather all the participants of the meeting, as an expression of group association.

The non-Indigenous – myself, members of the Alagoas rural union and members of movements against the transposition of the São Francisco River – hurried back to our tents, set up under the central hut of the indigenous territory in the Caatinga – protected from the weather. At the same time and inversely, the Indigenous peoples of diverse groups ran to the "terreiro" in front of our tents and began to sing and dance the Toré. The fire bravely resisted the abundance of rainwater.

We, the non-Indigenous, remained comfortably inside the hut, talking about the issues raised throughout the meeting. The conversation lasted a long time— we hoped that the rite would end soon. We lacked the courage both to participate and to admit our lack.

The circle did not end! The Indigenous danced in the rain, covered in mud, all night long.

I did not see the end of the rite.

I slept thinking about the images of those mingling bodies, smiling in the light of the fire. Thinking about that other Caatinga.

All of them, the Indigenous, the Caatinga, ideas, mud, joy, birds, fire, laughter, flowers, sounds, water, laughter... associated, interconnected, forming a special, musical and exciting landscape. Neither past suffering nor the mysterious future existed anymore. Nor did desertification. There was life!

Life in the Caatinga was that moment a life of joy and jubilation. Always.

References

Kamêr, Júlio Ribeiro Apinajé, Alexandre Herbetta. 2008. *Cantos filosóficos e a possibilidade de uma pluriversidade*. Goiânia: Revista Articulando e Construindo.

Wallerstein, Immanuel. 2005. *Las incertidumbres del saber*. Barcelona: Editorial Gedisa.

32 instrucciones para escuchar con/en una epidemia global

RUI CHAVES es artista sonoro, intérprete e investigador portugués. Su trabajo creativo pone en primer plano una discusión sobre la presencia física del fenómeno del sonido así como la suya como autor en el proceso de producción de arte sonoro, basada en una investigación crítica del cuerpo, el lugar, el texto y la tecnología. Entre 2015 y 2018 fue investigador postdoctoral en NuSom (Universidad de São Paulo) con un proyecto centrado en la creación de un archivo digital de arte sonoro brasileño. En 2019, co-edita junto a Fernando Iazzetta el volumen *Making it Heard: A History of Brazilian Sound Art* (Bloomsbury). Actualmente es profesor internacional invitado en la Universidad Federal de Paraíba.

1. Introducción

32 instruções para escutar n(a) pandemia es un proyecto editorial[1] surgido de la contribución de un grupo de artistas sonoros brasileños que respondieron al desafío curatorial de considerar el sonido como una pieza del sistema sensible que necesariamente atiende tópicos como la soledad, la intimidad, el deseo, la separación, el encuentro, el dolor y la felicidad. Se trata de un manual compuesto por textos e imágenes que permite la interferencia poética y/o directa del lector-oyente (Fig. 1), y consta de un tiraje de cien ejemplares. La investigación ahonda en mi enfoque poético y conceptual, que se basa en el doloroso presente histórico y político de Brasil para reflexionar sobre el sonido como una forma de transitar de un pasado distópico a un momento utópico. Un arte sonoro que genere una arritmia / ritmia productiva entre el tiempo del cuerpo, el tiempo de la vida cotidiana y el tiempo del capitalismo[2].

---

[1] El proyecto es el resultado de una colaboración con el Prof. Fernando Iazzetta (Universidade de São Paulo) y contó con la participación de Bella, Camila Proto, Flora Holderbaum, Gabriela Mureb, Gustavo Torres, Inés Terra, Julia Teles, Laura Leiner, Laura Mello, Lílian Campesato, Lilian Nakao Nakahodo, Marcelo Armani, Marco Scarassatti, Mariana Carvalho, Paulo Dantas, Pontogor, Raquel Stolf, Ricardo Basbaum, Romano, Sérgio Abdalla, Tânia Neiva, Tati Cocteau, Thessia Machado, Thiago Ruiz, Tom Nóbrega, Valéria Bonafé, Valério Fiel da Costa, Vanessa De Michelis, Yuri Bruscky.

[2] Me inspira la idea de ritmo-análisis propuesta por Henri Lefebvre (2004).

> Rasga as instruções
>
> Abre a tua janela
>
> Escuta o voo

Fig.1. *Prefácio. Rui Chaves [c2021]. 32 instruções para escutar n(a) pandemia.* [Romper las instrucciones // Abre tu ventana // Escucha el vuelo].

De manera similar al enraizamiento simultáneo de la membrana basilar en múltiples ubicaciones, cada instrucción dibuja un momento: el ausentarse de uno mismo para escuchar al otro y devolver un yo-nosotros (Fig. 2), el pensar poéticamente ya no el silencio-disciplina sino el silencio-entre, el presente en el siempre frágil acto de la conversación (Figura 3), el cultivo de la contemplación productiva de

Escutar com máxima
concentração as
porosidades da pedra
e as lâminas
cortantes do sol

Fig.2. Instrução nº4. Ale Fenerich [c2021]. 32 instruções para escutar n(a) pandemia.

[Escucha con maximo // concentración en // porosidades de piedra // y las cuchillas // objetos punzantes del sol].

Fig. 3. Instrução nº2. SOU TODA OUVIDOS (versão 8). Raquel Stolf [c2021]. 32 instruções para escutar n(a) pandemia. [Soy toda oídos].

SOU TODA OUVIDOS

Escuto gratuitamente silêncios impossíveis, *ex-possíveis* e incompossíveis, por telefone e/ou mensagem. 43-984234419

> [Lento]
> meditar alterações degenerativas
> .
> .
> ao sinal de desgaste, assobiar
> .
> gritar conforme grau de erosão
> rir conforme grau de desvio
> [fermata]
> ecoar nos espaços de articulações
> pausar nas fissuras emocionais
> .
> .
> [presto]
> ligamentos devem ser repercutidos
> fraturas, expostas sem dó
> [da capo, quantas vezes quiser]

Fig. 4. Instrução nº12. Partitura radiográfica para sobreviver a um ano em luxação. Lilian Nakao Nakahodo [c2021]. 32 instruções para escutar n(a) pandemia. [(Lento) meditar cambios degenerativos / a la señal de desgaste, silbar / gritar según el grado de erosión reír según el grado de desviación (fermata) eco en espacios articulares pausa en los antojos emocionales / (presto) los ligamentos deben resonar fracturas expuestas sin piedad (da capo, tantas veces como quieras)].

nuestro bienestar psíquico (Fig. 4), el pensamiento de hacer-son fuera del signo hegemónico de la institución-disciplina, o el ejercicio de pensar el sonido como una interpelación preñada de significados para otro mundo-comunidad posible.

Los actos de escucha descritos en este texto son formas de resistencia en una coyuntura histórica que separa, deshumaniza y estigmatiza cada vez más a las personas que intentan *el buen vivir*. Ejemplo de ello es que —con la supuesta intención de proteger a los niños contra la pedofilia— el parlamento húngaro aprobó la ley 157-1, un paquete legislativo que prohíbe a los medios de comunicación locales y al sistema

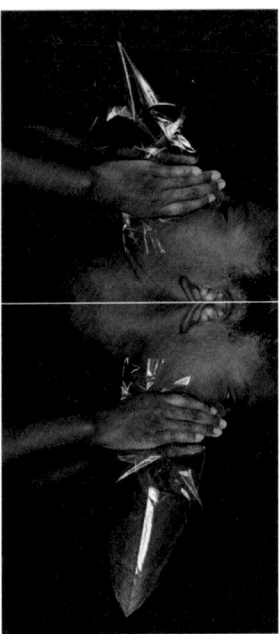

Fig. 5. *Instrução nº27. RESPIRO.* Paola Ribeiro. [c2021]. *32 instruções para escutar n(a) pandemia.*

educativo representar y defender la voz y el espacio de personas *queer* y transexuales (Rankin 2021). Lo son también los cientos de refugiados intentando entrar en el enclave español de Ceuta (Boaziz 2021): escuchamos su desesperación cuando llegan demacrados vía marítima y son recibidos por la policía antidisturbios, que protege con violencia la *pureza* de un continente antiguo y desesperanzado. Esta obsesión por la necropolítica y por la represión de la felicidad de los demás se vuelve entonces paradójica cuando la vida se interrumpe prematuramente para tantos millones de personas[3], y el dolor empaña

---

3 Al momento de escribir este artículo, COVID-19 ha cobrado la vida de más de 500.000 personas en Brasil: https://coronavirus.jhu.edu/region/brazil

la mucha existencia individual y la poca existencia colectiva que queda.

2. Motivación

En 31 *instruções para escutar n(a) pandemia* defiendo un pensamiento no esencialista con respecto al sonido[4]: además de ser un fenómeno físico, el sonido está cargado de polisemia y existe también en su ausencia, particularmente cuando participa de la regulación de los cuerpos. En este ensayo propongo que la discusión salga del idealismo y se instale en el materialismo contradictorio, lejos del dualismo exclusivo y reductivo que opone el blanco al negro, el silencio al ruido, la música a la no música, la visión al oído o, como diría Murray Schafer, «Hi-Fi» y «Lo-Fi» (1993). De esta forma, el compositor canadiense puede abogar —como uno de los caminos hacia un *tuning of the world*— por un regreso a una época preindustrial, a una aldea global no contaminada por el imperialismo de los sonidos mecánicos. Sin embargo lo cierto es que de haber existido este lugar también hubiera estado sujeto al colonialismo y la esclavitud, pues es evidente que hay utilidad en el pensamiento estructuralista, como señala Karl Marx acera de la manera en la que el trabajo de la mayoría es capitalizado por una ínfima fracción de la sociedad, el 1%.

---

[4] Más detalles en *Making Oneself Heard in Public, through Art and in Sound-Based Scholarship* (Chaves 2019).

Pero la clase no es lo único que oprime la existencia humana. Ante el peligro de una teoría general o unitaria de las cosas conviene impulsar el proceso de nostalgia, es decir, el regreso a un cierto pasado idealizado. *Terra Brasilis* no es el mito de los pobres felices y emprendedores capaces de revertir su condición —siempre y cuando no sean perezosos, ni negros, claro—. Antes de la pandemia, la Organización Mundial de la Salud mostró a Brasil como un país serio en cuanto al cuidado de la salud mental, a pesar de los doce millones de personas que padecieron depresión entre 2017 y 2018. La mortalidad del virus se vio entonces amplificada por un biocapital que ya restaba vitalidad a muchos cuerpos —a través de un urbanismo obsesionado con la fábula del crecimiento eterno, que contrasta con la realidad de las vidas incrustadas en guetos, alejadas de los centros de poder y de la toma de decisiones.

La represión policial y los habituales mensajes de terror y crimen vulgarizan al *homo bandidus* y veneran al *homo milicianos*. Un sujeto, que disfruta vestirse de camuflaje o de negro, que usa el «dialecto» carioca y siente nostalgia por la dictadura militar, se siente convocado al debate sobre una pandemia al tiempo que le enorgullece desconocer la diferencia entre un protozoo y un virus. Más comúnmente llamado «milico», este sujeto ve falos en logotipos institucionales[5] y critica la búsqueda de la verdad sobre el asesinato de Marielle Franco[6]. Y más recientemente, este espécimen protagonizó una violenta acción policial que provocó la muerte de veintisiete personas en la favela de *Jacarézinho*, donde se concentra la mayor población negra (Mercer 2021). Este macabro acto coincidió con el despliegue de una comisión investigadora parlamentaria, impulsada por un grupo de seguidores de la oposición en el senado federal, y que se centra en las acciones del gobierno de Bolsonaro en el combate a la pandemia. En las semanas posteriores a la masacre, una manifestación pacífica en la capital de Pernambuco, Recife, fue atacada por un contingente policial con balas de goma, que causó la ceguera en dos transeúntes (Sobreira 2021).

Al momento de escribir este artículo, el discurso negacionista —cuyo principal defensor es el presidente— queda expuesto en su negativa[7] a usar la

---

[5] En 2021, por iniciativa del Senado brasileño, se estableció una comisión parlamentaria con el fin de esclarecer las acciones del gobierno federal en el combate a la crisis de salud. Una de las personas invitadas fue Mayra Pinheiro, miembro del gobierno de Bolsonaro en el área de salud. Durante su testimonio, el senador Randolfe Rodrigues presentó un audio en que ella muestra su indignación por haber visto un supuesto 'pene' dentro de la reconocida institución de salud pública, Fundação Oswaldo Cruz. Durante la sesión se aclaró que el 'pene' visto era un logo institucional de la fundación.

[6] Declaración hecha por Mayra Pinheiro en el mismo áudio.

[7] El presidente Bolsonaro a menudo aparece desenmascarado.

mascarilla (Krüger 2021) y a respetar la directriz de mantener distancia social, aludiendo que tenemos que afrontar la situación como «hombres» (n.d. 2020) y haciendo público su temor a convertirse en un caimán a casua de la vacuna contra la COVID-19 (Alfano 2021). Asimismo, ordenó a sus subordinados a interpretar fuera de tono el Ave María de Charles Gounod en honor a las víctimas de la COVID-19 (Pinheiro 2020), y silenció periodistas —especialmente mujeres (Lemos 2021). En suma, el milico se considera un macho alfa, y es una persona mezquina y cobarde que odia lo contradictorio.

3. A (des)união?

Quizás mi descripción poco halagadora del milico caiga en una polarización que dificulta la empatía, así como el ejercicio de escuchar y ser escuchado. Pero cabe decir que concuerdo con las discusiones sobre la importancia de la esfera pública y la pertinencia de que las demandas de los diferentes grupos sociales serán reconocidos, así como en la existencia de valores comunes compartidos. Tengo la esperanza de que, en su muy limitado campo de acción, *31 instruções para escutar n(a) pandemia* pueda leerse como un impulso contra el bloque de acciones autoritarias y políticamente represivas que sucedieron no solo en el contexto de la pandemia, sino que precedieron a la elección del actual jefe de

Estado. Contra el eterno retorno del conservadurismo que inspecciona la producción artística, demoniza las instituciones democráticas, hace apología de la violencia simbólica y física contra el otro, y desprestigia cualquier alternativa al modelo neoliberal. Esta melodía tiene una dimensión afectiva que busca trastocar nuestra vida pública, y acercarla a un colectivo que permanezca abierto al disenso y la contradicción, mantiendiendo al márgen aquella represión orgánica excluyente que sueña con una entropía conservadora reacia al cambio.Retornando al esencialismo, soy crítico de discurso(s) en los que la estética opere como un catalizador aceleracionista. De hecho, esperar una transformación sistémica que resulte del descubrimiento de los límites del capitalismo es análogo a la tesis de la inmunidad colectiva. Eventualmente llegaremos allí, pero en el camino morirán millones de personas. En la estetización actual de la política, donde el ascenso de los *homo milicianos* es el protagonista de una inversión evolutiva o el paso del bipedismo al cuadrupedismo, en un enciclopedismo obsesionado con la primacía del buey sobre la preservación del medio ambiente, resulta pertinente la publicación de obras que participen de otros sistemas de afecto y cuidados.

Referencias

Alfano, Bruno. 2021 "Veja sete vezes em que Bolsonaro desestimulou vacinas contra a Covid-19", O Globo, 23 de marzo de 2021. https://oglobo.globo.com/sociedade/vacina/veja-sete-vezes-em-que-bolsonaro-desestimulou-vacinas-contra-covid-19-24938536.

Bouaziz, Fatima. 2021. "Thousands of Migrants Head for Ceuta from Morocco", Atalayar, 30 de junio de 2021. https://atalayar.com/en/content/thousands-migrants-head-ceuta-morocco.

Chaves, Rui. 2019. "Making Oneself Heard in Public, through Art and in Sound-Based Scholarship" en Making it Heard: A History of Brazilian Sound Art. Rui Chaves, Fernando Iazzetta (eds.). New York: Bloomsbury Academic, 43-70.

Estadão Conteúdo. 2020. "Bolsonaro diz que é preciso 'enfrentar vírus como homem e não como moleque'", en ISTOÉ Independente. https://istoe.com.br/bolsonaro-diz-que-e-preciso-enfrentar-virus-como-homem-e-nao-como-moleque/.

John Hopkins Hospital University. 2021. "Brazil - COVID-19 Overview - Johns Hopkins", Johns Hopkins Coronavirus Resource Center. https://coronavirus.jhu.edu/region/brazil.

Lefebvre, Henri. 2004. Rhythmanalysis: Space, Time, and Everyday Life. London: New York: Continuum.

Lemos, Nina. 2021. "Opinião: Nina Lemos - Bolsonaro tem predileção por maltratar jornalistas mulheres", consultado el 5 de julio de 2021. https://www.uol.com.br/universa/colunas/nina-lemos/2021/06/21/gritos-com-reporter-provam-que-bolsonaro-e-presidente-abusivo.htm.

Mercier, Daniela. 2021. "Polícia insiste em criminalização de vítimas de massacre do Jacarezinho, mas recua sobre 29a morte", EL PAÍS, 8 de mayo de 2021. https://brasil.elpais.com/brasil/2021-05-08/mortos-na-chacina-do-jacarezinho-sobem-para-29-e-policia-insiste-na-criminalizacao-de-vitimas-sem-provas.html.

Oliveira, Mayara. 2020. "Ao lado de sanfoneiro, Bolsonaro presta homenagem às vítimas do coronavírus", Metrópoles, 26 de junio de 2020. https://www.metropoles.com/brasil/politica-brasil/ao-lado-de-sanfoneiro-bolsonaro-presta-homenagem-as-vitimas-do-coronavirus.

Rankin, Jennifer. 2021. "Hungary Passes Law Banning LGBT Content in Schools or Kids' TV", The Guardian, 15 de junio de 2021. http://www.theguardian.com/world/2021/jun/15/hungary-passes-law-banning-lbgt-content-in-schools.

Schafer, R. Murray. 1993. The Soundscape: Our Sonic Environment and the Tuning of the World. Rochester, Vt.: [United States]: Destiny Books.

Sobreira, Vinicius. 2021. "Repressão em Pernambuco acende alerta e movimentos falam em 'fascistização' da PM", Brasil de Fato, 04 de junio de 2021. https://www.brasildefato.com.br/2021/06/04/repressao-em-pernambuco-acende-alerta-e-movimentos-falam-em-fascistizacao-da-pm.

Krüger, Ana. "Em dia de recorde de mortes, Bolsonaro questiona o uso de máscaras", Congresso em Foco, 25 de febrero de 2021. https://congressoemfoco.uol.com.br/governo/em-dia-de-recorde-de-mortes-bolsonaro-questiona-o-uso-de-mascaras/.

World Health Organization. 2017. "Depression and Other Common Mental Disorders: Global Health Estimates". https://apps.who.int/iris/handle/10665/254610.

Listening for Alida Vázquez: A Life in Electronic Music between Migration, Race and Gender

TERESA DÍAZ DE COSSIO is a flutist, a DMA student at UC San Diego, and flute teacher at *Universidad Autónoma de Baja California*. Díaz de Cossio has been inclined to reach out for meaningful engagements with communities through her creative practice from the beginning of her musical endeavors, firstly through *Música para la Paz*, and now as the coordinator of *Neofonía, Festival de Música Nueva*, Ensenada. Díaz de Cossio's present research examines the life and work of the composer, teacher, and pianist Alida Vázquez Ayala (1923-2015) and explores how Vázquez navigated race, gender and transnational networks in her teaching, performance and compositional work between Mexico and New York.

This article examines the life and work of the composer, teacher, and pianist Alida Vázquez Ayala (1923-2015) and explores how Vázquez navigated race, gender, and transnational networks in her work between Mexico and New York, and the Columbia Princeton Electronic Music Center (CPEMC). The investigation is based on oral history from CPEMC figures such as Kitty Brazelton (b.1951), Eric Chasalow (b.1955), alcides lanza (b.1929), Carlos Rausch (b.1924) and Pril Smiley (b.1943), friends such as Gloria Steinem (b.1934), Gena Raps (b.1941), and Jeannie Pool (b.1951), and Vázquez's nephews Jorge (b.1945) and Alejandro Martínez Vázquez (b.1947). The archives of the Women Philharmonic Orchestra and Institute for the Study of Women in Music have provided scores and recordings of Vázquez's works.

These sources are crucial because, other than 45 photographs, most of Vázquez's personal belongings were disposed of at the end of her life as those around her were not aware of the significance of her creative work. Vázquez is currently unknown in the narrative of Mexican American performers or composers, and I only learned about her by coincidence a year ago, upon reading Esperanza Pulido's chapter on Mexican women composers from 1983:

> Among current Mexican women composers of fine art music, Alida Vázquez, who became an American

citizen but never forgot Mexico, is undoubtedly the best-prepared. She is now finishing her dissertation at Columbia University, where she has been studying for two years and has won several grants and a prize. She studied electronic music with Davidovsky and Ussachevsky. Some of her already-performed compositions are *Suite for the Piano, Electronic Moods and Piano Sounds, Acuarelas de México for Voice and Piano, Piece for Clarinete and Piano.*

Esperanza Pulido's paragraph prompts critical elements to start reconstructing Vázquez's life and work, to which will be circling back in this paper. Pulido also reminds us of the challenges faced by women composers, particularly in Mexico:

> To understand the very belated acceptance of Mexican women as composers and performers and in other intellectual areas, one should be aware of at least two facts: a certain atavism and an undesirable male trait. Both held a grip on women for centuries. They are known as *malinchismo* and *machismo*.

These challenges remain relevant to the reality faced by Vázquez. Through her history, we will learn about some of the problematic situations she faced as a woman and the diverse techniques used to respond to the oppressive system she and other women musicians encountered.

Early years in Mexico City (1931–1948): Influences on the beginning of her musical journey

Vázquez's childhood and early musical education took place in Mexico City. Born to a family of three daughters, her father, Mateo Sergio Vázquez was a freemason. Her mother Rosalia Ayala was an avid singer, who was expelled from the house and separated from her family in the early years of her daughters' lives.[1] Nevertheless, their mother's voice seems to have remained in the memories of the three girls, and Vázquez and her sister Dora found ways to connect singing to all aspects of their lives. Vázquez sang while accompanying herself on the guitar, conducted a choir in a church, and song influenced her compositions, always lyrical in style and quality, ranging from serialism to polytonality. The sisters were raised by her freemason father, from whom they learned kindness, as shown in Vázquez's care for those around her (including homeless animals), and a sense of self-improvement. These aspects informed her feminist ideas and drove her desire to pursue graduate degrees in her forties.

As a child, Vázquez was enrolled at the *Conservatorio Nacional de Música* in Mexico City. Vázquez met Claudio Arrau at this institution—impressed with her piano abilities, the Chilean pianist took Vázquez under his wing and brought her to New York City in 1948. The connection with Arrau and the Jewish Community built important bridges for Vázquez; among them, by means of Arrau's friendship with pianist and contemporary music expert

---

[1] Jorge and Alejandro Martínez Vázquez, interview by author, telephone, June 10, 2020.

Grete Sultan. Later, in the 1970s, Sultan became a good friend and mentor to Vázquez during a key period in which Sultan collaborated with John Cage and taught pupils such as Christian Wolff and Lucia Dlugoszewski. The importance of this friendship can be seen in Vázquez's dedication to Sultan of her 1974 septet.

<u>Life in New York City, introduction to feminism: Taking on music education, networking among women</u>

In a life driven by curiosity and persistence, Vázquez broke expectations. During her first decade in New York, Vázquez explored new avenues for music education. In the early years following her arrival, she studied piano with Claudio Arrau, Dalcroze method and improvisation at the Diller-Quaile Music School between 1948 and 1951, and music and dance therapy with Marian Chace in the early 1950's. Years later, Vázquez met Gena Raps, who was a colleague at Mannes, and they became close friends. Raps has this to say about Vázquez's approach to teaching: "She had a very unique way of teaching and her own system of teaching theory. Mannes was very famous for its theory program, and she was not teaching [sic] that way... she was an outsider wherever she was, she was an outsider at Mannes, and she was an outsider at Columbia, because she had her own way of doing things."[2] This determination, here observed between 1964 and 1974, left a profound mark on Vázquez's life a decade later when she was working on her DMA.

Raps says that she and Vázquez became friends because both "were arch-feminists and bonded as feminists. We all knew that we were not able to make the careers that we wanted to make—you know, she was close to Gloria." Raps refers here to Gloria Steinem, a friend and neighbor of Vázquez at 73rd St who became a kind of a family during Vázquez's last years, serving as her legal guardian. When interviewing Steinem, she remarked that Vázquez was "very devoted to music –its teaching and composing." Steinem also noted regarding equality: "I had the impression that she and other women musicians and composers were marginalized when compared with their male counterparts… She once invited me to go with her to a large conference of women composers, and it was the first time I glimpsed their numbers and all their problems of getting their work performed by symphony orchestras."[3] The conference in question was the *International Congress for Women Composers* (ICWM), an event that took place in 1981, led by Jeannie Pool, another of Vázquez's friends.

---

[2] Gena Raps, interview by author, telephone, February 12, 2021.

[3] Gloria Steinem, interview by author, email, October 19, 2020.

Another important friend was Esperanza Pulido. The director of *Heterofonía,* a Journal in Mexico, Pulido published Vázquez's scores and letters, feeling there was a gap in recognition for Mexican composers. Jeannie Pool described Esperanza as "the spiritual mother" of many Mexican composers and a kind, generous, and loving woman. The friendship of strong women had a long-lasting influence on Vázquez; they understood feminism as a culture and created networks of support and empathy among each other.

A new journey as a composer: Institutions, aesthetics, and Mexican heritage

In 1966, Vázquez was 35, a woman with an established career as a piano and music theory teacher at the preparatory program of Mannes School. That summer, claiming she was tired of playing other people's music, she composed her first work,[4] a piano suite in four movements: *Allemande, Courante, Sarabande and Gigue*. The movements have a binary form, adhering to the baroque tradition, and the piece's total length is eight minutes. Dynamic markings were added later. Between 1966 and 1973, Vázquez composed seven pieces ranging from string quartets to solo piano works, duets, and vocal works. These works were performed at different

---
4 Naomi Lehman, interview by author, telephone, May 14, 2020.

venues, such as the Benning Composers Conference, the New York City Town Hall, or the Mannes School.

Following her desire to study composition, Vázquez pursued a master's program in music composition under the tutelage of Mario Davidovsky at City College from 1973 to 1976. In her thesis, Vázquez outlines the three movements of her string quartet no. 2 from 1975, emphasizing the continuity achieved "without the help of a principal tonal center and other adjacent ones." It is important to point out that the vocabulary Vázquez uses to describe her music is free of gender associations, and focuses on describing technical elements. Only in the very last paragraph does Vázquez speak of her influence: "I am aware that certain aspects of this quartet indicate my Mexican heritage. This is particularly evident in the first movement through the rhythmic patterns and the natural ease of the changing meter." Overall, Vázquez's vocabulary and discursive strategy give us a glimpse into her conception of music and pinpoints the importance of rhythm in her work. Vázquez used rhythmic patterns to connect new vocabularies, such as polytonality and serialism, with her Mexican heritage as expressed in her music's rhythmic quality. Rhythm holds a very important place among the compositional elements Vázquez used, an element that she would still be referring to a decade later, as an tool for expressing herself.

The String Quartet no.2 was premiered at Columbia in 1975, with Harvey Sollberger directing, a contact perhaps facilitated by Davidovsky. Thereafter, between 1977 and 1984, Vázquez pursued the degree of Doctor of Music Arts at the Columbia-Princeton Electronic Music Center (CPEMC). While completing the coursework and writing a thesis project for the DMA, Vázquez also taught the use of the equipment to undergraduate students as a Teaching Assistant. Vázquez supported herself by working as an organist and conducting the choir at the Church "Smokey Mary," while teaching and studying at Columbia.

Alongside Vázquez, other Latin American Students arrived through outreach efforts of CPEMC professors such as Ussachevsky and Davidovsky. They traveled more than once to El Centro Latinoamericano de Altos Estudios Musicales (CLAEM) in Argentina. alcides lanza was among the students who walked the path between CLAEM and the CPEMC. In 1965, after arriving at the CPEMC, alcides wrote "Interferences I," using the same instruments that the group in Downton were using at that time, and handed it to the directors of the Contemporary Music Group of Columbia University. The piece wasn't performed, and alcides described this as a local problem: uptown versus downtown.[5] Referring to the aesthetic and geographical division

---

5 alcides lanza, interview by author, email, June 20, 2020.

that took place in Manhattan starting in 1960, the uptown scene focused on the academic music created by composers at Juilliard, the Manhattan School of Music and Columbia, while the downtown scene consisted of experimental composers and their works. Vázquez moved between the uptown and downtown scenes, with her connections to Columbia and the CPEMC; but continued her piano lessons with Grete Sultan in parallel while a student at Columbia.

The CPEMC seems to have had fairly clear aesthetic expectations of its students and allowed them a certain creative freedom at Columbia. For example, Carlos Rausch and Kitty Brazelton were graduate students at Columbia University during the late '70s and '80s, respectively. Discussing the matter with them, both mentioned that there were unspoken rules about aesthetics they had to follow, and Rausch referred to "aprender lo que nadie le dice" ("learn what nobody talks about"). [6]

At the CPEMC, Pril Smiley was both a composer and an instructor at the Center. Smiley was also one of Vázquez's mentors, teaching her the technical side of the equipment, which was not digital at the time and didn't yet involve synthesizers. Smiley taught Vázquez how to splice tapes, use the recording machines, use the tape recorders, and supplied her with tape. Smiley recalls Vázquez was one of the first

---

6 Carlos Rausch, interview by author, telephone, May 2020.

female composers studying in the electronic music field at CPEMC— one of her few contemporaries was Ursula Mamlock. Smiley remembers Vázquez as short in stature, always using a little footstool, about ten inches high, underneath the tape recording consoles, moving it around to work with the mixing channel or the tape recorder. The footstool somehow became part of Vázquez's charm. Smiley had this to say in regards to Vázquez's personality:

> A charming person with a great sense of humor... A great composer, she was a great combination, a wonderful personality, because she was very, very serious and she felt like every minute, all the time she spent in the studio it was a privilege, to be there and be able to have this sound research, and she soaked up as much learning as she could.[7]

Eric Chasalow, Vázquez's classmate at Columbia, knew Vázquez as a friend and as part of the group of students from the CPEMC. He remembers her as one of the few women working in the studio:

> "I would show up and she would be you know, this is a very gendered thing... is that the men who used the studio would be like, just leave stuff all over the place and Alida would clean things up and curse at the men, you know, and say, why do you guys leave all this stuff around? And I would agree with her because it was terrible."[8]

In 1977 Vázquez created *Electronic Moods and Piano Sounds*, a piece for piano and electronics. Pril Smiley helped to deconstruct how the electronic

---
7 Pril Smiley, interview by the author, December 6, 2020.

8 Eric Chasalow, interview by the author, November 19, 2020.

sounds were created by the machines available in the studio in this work:

1) A white noise generator and sound wave generators were used as the source material to produce pitches, especially the sine wave generators.

2) To modify the sounds, various sound-multiplication devices were used to create textures, band-pass filters, envelope controls (to "chop" the sounds into rhythms), and an echo chamber.

3) Additionally, "classical analog studio" tape recording techniques were used, including speed control, backward playback, and feedback loops.[9]

Collaborations with dance and her DMA thesis project

In 1977, Vázquez was finishing her DMA at Columbia and working on her thesis, a collaboration with the dancer and choreographer Claudia Gitelman. Vázquez won a grant from the National League of American Pen Women Inc to realize the project. In her application, Vázquez wrote:

> I finished the work last year under the supervision of Prof. Jack Beeson at Columbia University; it consists of a small group of orchestral dances. Aware of my interest in dance music, Prof. Beeson suggested putting in a complete ballet for my thesis. For this, I contacted the dancer and choreographer Claudia

---

[9] Pril Smiley, interview (email) by the author, February 22, 2021

Gitelman. We have both agreed on the immediate need to have the ballet performed and recorded (once complete) so that the dancers can listen to the music. For this purpose, I propose to use the grant. For my work, I will use the traditional orchestra and electronic music. The latter I will compose at Columbia University under the direction of Mario Davidovsky. Later I will seek additional help to produce the ballet.

The prize of 1,000 dollars allowed Vázquez's graduation project to be realized.[10]

Vázquez described the experience of the composition process for electronic works to Esperanza Pulido in a letter from September 1979:

> It has been most fantastic, in terms of all the problems and possibilities of dance music and dance. It has been a great experience to discuss with her [Claudia Gitelman] and entirely depends on natural electronic sounds to complete a music structure with form and everything. I am gradually discovering and organizing a visual and more exact way of notating electronic music, which is very important - I have an insatiable concern about the form of music in contemporary music. I don't know if I thanked you, that from Mexico, you have a genuine interest in what I am doing. It has given me much courage. Thanks again.

A courage that was needed for what would follow. It's important to recall that Gena Raps observed that Vázquez had her own way of doing things; and elaborated by turning to Vázquez's work at the CPEMC:

> And I don't know if she ever completed her PhD because they had asked her to do it a specific way and

---

10 Pulido, Esperanza. 1980. *Cartas: Una compositora de grandes méritos*. Heterofonía. April-May-June, 1980.

she was not going to do it their way. So do you know
if she ever got it? I know she did a lot of work for it. I
know she was quite frustrated because she had put in
all that energy to take all the courses. And then when
it came to doing the dissertation at the paper, you
know, they turned her down and she was very, very
frustrated about that.[11]

Jeannie Pool offered another striking account:

Alida always had a gift for melody that meant they
really didn't like her because she was very sentimen-
tal and wrote music of the heart, so even when she
was trying to meet their demands her melodic gift
came out and they were just really against melody.
I think she was discriminated against because of
her age, she spoke with an accent, and she was very
definitely a Mexican American woman in her 40s in
the 1970s.[12]

This melodic intuition that Jeannie Pool is referring to permeated Vázquez's electronic works. While I do not have accounts from her committee, her friends point towards a rejection of her dissertation project. Vázquez's last year at the CPEMC was 1984, and she stopped composing afterwards. When Jeannie Pool was asked why, her answer was, "what I loved about it was that she didn't get cynical, and she was just always "well, that's where it is, let's do our best", she was always like that and later in life it be-came just overwhelming to her…I mean, how much

---

11 Gena Raps, interview by author, telephone, February 12, 2021.

12 Jeannie Pool, interview by author, zoom, February 11, 2021.

discouragement can you endure?" The same year, Vázquez stated in a Mexican newspaper in 1984, "Now I no longer adhere to any of these techniques [serialism to polytonal] – I try to express what I feel with my own style. I have composed many works in which my Mexican origins are recognizable, especially in the rhythms."

In 1984 the International Congress of Women Musicians took place in Mexico City. In this environment foregrounding women, Vázquez flourished: she moderated panels, conducted her own works, led presentations on electronic music, helped with administrative work and did translations of newspaper articles or reviews in Spanish. This network of feminist activists and artists enabled Vázquez to become part of efforts to create spaces that portrayed the work of women composers. After the congress, in a Mexican Newspaper Vázquez wrote:

> It is of great importance that women participate in the field of music, but unfortunately, there are very few opportunities for them. However, we are struggling to obtain a prominent position in this branch of the Beaux Arts. The importance of this nature, asserting that this international movement of Women In Music which was initiated by Jeannie Pool has extended itself far and wide: consequently, there now exists an exchange of ideas, knowledge, and instruction pertaining to the 'universal language': music... My heart is brimming with pride because to be in my country listening to my music is the utmost gratification.[13]

---
13 Pool, Jeanie. 2009. Passions of Musical Women: The Story of The International Congress on Women In Music. La Cresenta: Jaygale Music.

Vázquez and other women composers faced conditions that challenged the inclusion of their works in a predetermined canon (Citron). The following outline put's Vázquez's life into perspective, especially her efforts to make a space for herself in the field of academic composition in New York during the 1970-80's:

1. She had access to diverse music education. Vázquez's first composition teacher was Bernard Wagenaar from the Juilliard School. She subsequently pursued graduate degrees at CCNY and Columbia, studying with Mario Davidovsky and Chou Wen-Chung, some of the foremost composers of their time.

2. Publication is key to keep music circulating and performed. Vázquez managed to publish her piece for Clarinet and Piano (1970), and Music for Seven Instruments (1974), both at Seesaw Music Corp, N.Y.

3. Performance of one's works and recording are important keys to bringing the music alive. Vázquez was able to get her music premiered and recorded at a range of venues in New York and Mexico City.

4. Most of Vázquez's works were for chamber ensembles, except her thesis project, which was an orchestral piece with electronics. According to

Marcia Citron, throughout history, "large forms tend to hold greater value than small forms."

5. Vázquez's music tended to be lyrical, including her thesis work which she may quite possibly have been asked to change for this reason.

Vázquez's age, and aesthetic voice, took her away from the dominant narratives of twenty-century composition, and her story deserves to be revived. For her flexibility to move in diverse aesthetics (both uptown and downtown scenes) and her unique voice that separated her from the canon at certain institutions. Vázquez's life and work may still be virtually unknown, but this article seeks to draw attention to her extraordinary efforts as both a Mexican American Women, and as a pioneer in electronic music.

References

Citron, M. J. (1993). *Gender and the musical canon*. Cambridge: Cambridge Univ. Press.

McClary, S. (1991). *Feminine endings: Music, gender, and sexuality*. Minneapolis: University of Minnesota Press.

Pool, Jeanie. 2009. *Passions of Musical Women: The Story of The International Congress on Women In Music*. La Cresenta: Jaygale Music.

Pulido, E. (1983). *Mexican Women in Music*. Latin American Music Review / Revista De Música Latinoamericana, 4(1), 120-131. doi:10.2307/780282

On Temperament and Tempering

REIKO YAMADA is a composer and sound artist, originally from Hiroshima, Japan. She composes concert works, creates sound art installations, and works with interdisciplinary collaborators. Her work explores the aesthetic concept of imperfection in a variety of contexts. Yamada holds a D.Mus. in composition from McGill University and is a recipient of numerous prestigious awards and fellowships including a Fellowship at the Radcliffe Institute for Advanced Study of Harvard University in 2016-16. She is currently a postdoctoral researcher at ICFO (Institute for Photonic Sciences) and composer-in-residence at the Phonos Foundation in Barcelona.

As a composer from Japan trained in the Western musical tradition, I sometimes have uneasy feelings about composing music in European styles. At the same time, I am also uncomfortable with the appropriation and exploitation of Asian cultural traditions, such as the traditional tuning systems (for example, Raga in Classical Indian Music or the pentatonic scales of Japanese *Shakuhachi* or *Gagaku* music), by both European and Asian composers. A recent project focused on artistic research and creation using the digital organs at the Zentrum für Orgelforschung der Kunstuniversität Graz gave me the opportunity, twenty years into my career, to reassess these relationships and examine the very foundation of Western music by exploring its historical tuning systems. This exploration, in turn, led me to draw inspiration from an aesthetic principle that originates in the Japanese musical tradition yet remains entirely within the vocabulary of Western music.

For centuries, Western musicians and scholars have tried to define the pitch relations within an octave by dividing it into twelve equally-spaced notes. A set of pitches that produce mathematical proportions between the fixed tones, or intervals, is known as a tuning system. However, splitting the octave into exact, equally-spaced steps while, at the same time, producing interval relations that are harmonically in tune is impossible. Thus, throughout the history of music, the complexity of this problem has bothered physicists, composers and music theorists, many of whom have proposed compromised solutions prioritizing either pure harmonic relations or equal distance between the twelve tones.

For example, *just intonation* is one of many historical Western tuning systems that focuses on purity as a way of preserving the harmonic order found in the natural world. This type of tuning involves arranging the main intervals as whole-number ratios (i.e., 3:2 or 4:3). Nonetheless, in just intonation, the pure sonorities of some intervals come at the cost of creating great discrepancies in others, hence producing so-called "wolf" intervals. A wolf interval is an interval that is notably sharper or flatter than the size of the corresponding justly-tuned interval (the result of tuning other intervals to be harmonically pure), and is therefore exceedingly dissonant, which sounds quite unpleasant. Countless variations of such tuning systems were developed by placing wolf intervals in various locations based on musical trends and ideological beliefs. The practice of tuning in harmonically pure intervals by one method or another, whether *just intonation* or *meantone temperaments*,[1] flourished during the Renaissance and Baroque

---

[1] To put it simply, while just intonation seeks to maintain the purity of the fifths, meantone tunings narrow the fifths in order to maintain the purity of the common thirds.

periods. Some of these systems continued to be used throughout the nineteenth century, alongside other, newly invented tuning systems.

In contrast, a system such as the twelve note *equal temperament*, developed in the eighteenth century and the most widely used tuning system in Western music today, does not prioritize the preservation of pure intonation. Instead, it proposes that an octave be divided into twelve equal semitones, avoiding the shocking wolf tone by slightly reducing all the intervals. However, this solution makes all intervals impure. Today, practically all Western instruments with *fixed pitches* are tuned using equal temperament.[2]

Interval	Example	Ratio	Just	ET	Bach WT	Sixth-Comma	55-Division
Minor Semitone	C–C♯	135:128	92.2	100	94-110	88.6	87.3
Major Semitone	C–D♭	16:15	111.7	100	94-110	108.2	109.1
Minor Tone	C–D	10:9	182.4	200	196-204	196.7	196.4
Major Tone	C–D	9:8	203.9	200	196-204	196.7	196.4
Diminished 3rd	C♯–E♭	256:225	223.5	200	196-204	216.3	218.2
Augmented 2nd	C–D♯	75:64	274.6	300	294-306	285.3	283.6
Minor 3rd	C–E♭	6:5	315.6	300	294-306	304.9	305.4
Major 3rd	C–E	5:4	386.3	400	392-406	393.5	392.7
Diminished 4th	C–F♭	32:25	427.4	400	392-406	413.4	414.6
Augmented 3rd	C–E♯	125:96	478.5	500	496-502	482.1	480.0
"Perfect" 4th	C–F	4:3	498.04	500	496-502	501.6	501.8
Augmented 4th	C–F♯	45:32	590.2	600	594-608	590.2	589.1
Diminished 5th	C–G♭	64:45	609.8	600	594-608	609.8	610.9
"Perfect" 5th	C–G	3:2	701.96	700	698-704	698.4	698.2
Augmented 5th	C–G♯	405:256	794.1	800	794-808	787.0	785.4
Minor 6th	C–A♭	8:5	813.7	800	794-808	806.5	807.3
Major 6th	C–A	5:3	884.4	900	894-906	895.1	894.6
Augmented 6th	C–A♯	225:128	976.5	1000	996-1004	983.7	981.8
Minor 7th (lesser)	C–B♭	16:9	996.1	1000	996-1004	1003.3	1003.6
Minor 7th (greater)	C–B♭	9:5	1017.6	1000	996-1004	1003.3	1003.6
Major 7th	C–B	15:8	1088.3	1100	1094-1106	1091.9	1090.9
Diminished 8ve	C–C♭	256:135	1107.8	1100	1094-1106	1111.4	1112.7
Augmented 7th	C-B♯	2025:1024	1180.4	1200	1200	1180.4	1178.2
8ve	C–C	2:1	1200.0	1200	1200	1200.0	1200.0

Notes: As with the two Ds and the two Bbs, there are other possible Just ratios for some of these intervals: for example, 25:24 for a smaller minor semitone (70.7c), 25:16 for an augmented fifth (772.6c), and 125:64 for an augmented seventh (1158.9c). In this table I have given intervals that come closer to our usual scale.

Figure 1. Excerpt from the project sketchbook by Reiko Yamada

2 A "fixed-pitch" instrument refers to an instrument on which the pitches are prepared beforehand and cannot be altered in the moment (i.e., piano, guitar) unlike, for example, the human voice or the violin.

In practice, absolute and true equal *temperament*[3]—or any system, for that matter—is technically unattainable. Circumstances preventing its achievement include the infinite variety of physical factors affecting an instrument's sonic production, such as the quality of the air (temperature, humidity), and the distracting effect of timbre and harmonic contents on human perception. The notion of pure intonation, which the Pythagoreans championed as inspired by the purity of the soul or the movements of celestial bodies, no longer enjoys currency. Seeking to preserve historical tuning systems is no longer a matter of sacred beliefs or a search for a pure acoustic phenomenon, yet there is growing interest in historic Western temperament, particularly with the recent development of technologies such as user-friendly tuning apps.[4]

Far more than a strictly musical choice, this popular interest in alternatives to the relatively simple standard twelve-note equal temperament system seems to connect to a much broader postmodern phenomenon of questioning the basic assumptions underlying society, politics and the economic system

---

[3] A temperament is a tuning system that compromises on pure intervals to accommodate other musical requirements, such as the capacity to modulate to multiple keys.

[4] Popular tuning apps such as Airyware Tuner, APTuner, and Cleartune have come to include presets of dozens of historical tuning systems in recent years.

under which we live. Factors far beyond musical aesthetics have been invoked as justification for the use of historical music systems; for some, their use signifies returning to a kind of natural order, whereas accepting equal temperament involves compromising ideals for practicality. For example, Terry Riley, discussing composer La Monte Young's use of just intonation, states that Young's work is "crafted in such an original profound manner as to make us feel that it is the product of a large unknown tradition, aged and mellowed over peaceful centuries of development and of whose shamanic wisdom he is the sole heir."[5] Riley continues, "Here, for the first time in Western music, we experience the full-blown metaphysical archetypes of the Far East that infuse the high classicism of Bali, Java, India, and China, borne aloft on a separate ray, a genuine new breath of devotion [...] this is truth". In *Harmonic Experience*, musician and theorist W.A. Mathieu concludes that "pure harmony is hard-wired," that "The forces that govern the production of overtones govern our ears also, and our ears' responses."[6]

※　　※　　※

---

[5] In the liner notes of "The Well-Tuned Piano" by La Monte Young (1987).

[6] Mathieu, William Allaudin. 1997. *Harmonic experience: Tonal harmony from its natural origins to its modern expression*. Simon and Schuster.

The study of historical tuning systems in the West has traditionally been the domain of a small number of academics and enthusiasts. Most people in the field of music are content to ignore the issue entirely, assuming equal temperament as the standard tuning of the Western twelve-note chromatic scale. Yet among those who do pay attention to it, debates are strikingly heated. Within a relatively niche group of early music theorists and, particularly, interpreters and historians, heated discussions rage on issues ranging from the legitimacy of well-known scholarly works (such as those of Jorgensen)[7] to the theory and practice of applying various tuning systems to actual instruments.[8]

Until well into the nineteenth century, several tuning systems coexisted in various parts of Europe, their respective merits and drawbacks heatedly debated.

---

7 Jorgensen, Owen H. 1991. *Tuning: containing the perfection of eighteenth-century temperament, the lost art of nineteenth-century temperament, and the science of equal temperament, complete with instructions for aural and electronic tuning.* Vol. 4. East Lansing, MI: Michigan State University Press. Some scholars have criticized Jorgensen for the limited sources and his eccentric terminology used.

8 There are several journals and online communities dedicated to discussions on tuning theory, composition, instrument building, software development and information about tuning-related events around the world, such as *Xenharmonikon: An Informal Journal of Experimental Music* (Frog Peak Music) and *1/1 The Journal of the Just Intonation Network* (the officers of Other Music, Inc., 1985-2007). In academic journals such as *Early Music* (Oxford University Press), temperament and tuning systems are recurring subjects.

Theorists and instrumental makers built keyboards with 19, 27, or 32 keys per octave with split keys, a movable keyboard, or between two and six rows of keyboards in order to preserve pure intervals. Some theorists and composers invented multiple tuning systems and used them for various instruments, sometimes adopting different systems for each composition. It was only after a lengthy struggle against strong ideological resistance that equal temperament gradually became accepted as the universal system. What supporters of equal temperament claimed, and what critics in turn feared, did indeed happen: human ears and minds adapted to the imperfect and impure intervals of modern-day equal temperament.

Composers are naturally quite attuned to these concerns and many have explored alternative tuning systems. Most of their interest in recent decades has centered around the use of microtonality based on equal temperament or non-Western systems. However, composers such as La Monte Young, Harry Partch, Lou Harrison and Wendy Carlos are known for working with alternative tuning systems, including historical Western ones.

Interestingly, a similar interest also animates an unexpected group of non-specialists. Among the new age and alternative music communities, some call for tuning instruments to A=432 Hz instead of the generally accepted reference frequency of A=440 Hz, claiming that this non-standard system has "healing" properties and that the standard system is part of a broader conspiracy against the people.[9] More relevant to the present article is the fact that proponents of this view show a growing interest in and appreciation for pure or just intonation.

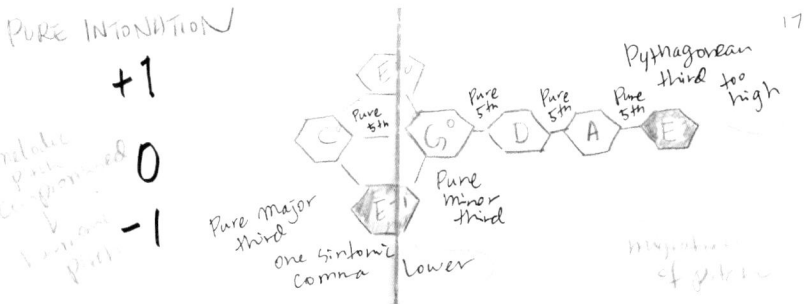

Figure 2. Excerpt from the project sketchbook by Reiko Yamada

---

9 Leonard G. Horowitz provides a good example of such conspiracy theory: "The monopolization of the music industry features this imposed frequency that is 'herding' populations into greater aggression, psychosocial agitation, and emotional distress predisposing people to physical illnesses and financial impositions profiting the agents, agencies, and companies engaged in the monopoly. Alternatively, the most natural, instinctively attractive, A=444Hz (C5=528Hz) frequency that is most vividly displayed botanically has been suppressed. That is, the 'good vibrations' that the plant kingdom obviously broadcasts in its greenish-yellow display, remedial to emotional distress, social aggression, and more, has been musically censored." (Horowitz, Leonard G. 2015. "Musical Cult Control: The Rockefeller Foundation's War on Consciousness Through the Imposition of A=440Hz Standard Tuning" in *Medical Veritas* 7.

With the recent development of easy-to-use tuning apps, several historical tuning systems containing pure intonations, previously effectively reserved for practitioners of so-called Early music (repertoire from Medieval, Renaissance and sometimes Baroque periods), suddenly became fashionable among non-academic musicians. Whether or not the definition and execution of historical tuning systems in the context of the new tools is historically accurate—or even properly implemented—is another question. In this context, equal temperament represents a powerful metaphor of an ideal compromised for the sake of practicality.

❀   ❀   ❀

Up until recently, I had mostly refrained from using alternative tuning systems, especially non-Western tuning systems, for one very simple reason: as an Asian composer, I wanted to avoid the cliché exoticism associated with non-Western tuning systems. I felt uncomfortable witnessing, over and over, the appropriation of Asian cultural traditions in various media in the West, the use of Asian tuning systems, such as those found in Japanese *shakuhachi* and *gagaku* music, by both European and Asian composers. Furthermore, as in many other Asian countries, Western music and the Western musical education system are now overwhelmingly dominant in Japan.

Almost all my musical education was based on the Western music system. The desire to counteract the disconnection this creates is what drove me, in 2016, to start exploring and reconsidering my relationship to European music in a radical way by deconstructing its very foundation, its tuning systems, and to do so at a European music institution.

While I was an artist-in-residence at IEM (Institute for Electronic Music and Acoustics), I started a project at the Zentrum für Orgelforschung der Kunstuniversität Graz (Center for Organ Research at University of Music and Performing Arts, Graz). The Organ Institute hosts, among other instruments, organs, keyboard and digital organs equipped with the Haptwerk and DynTune systems.[10] The DynTune system is a tool that allows organ players to switch the tuning system in real-time using a foot pedal. One of the organs equipped with the DynTune system was a hybrid organ developed by the company Rodgers Organs using a technology that combines a pipe organ with a digital organ, incorporating sample sets of historic pipe organs and offering cutting-edge digital capabilities. This instrument can be connected to loudspeakers using 24.2 channels instead of only sounding through the organ pipes.

---

10 DynTune, developed by Jan Ročnik, allows performers to make real-time modifications of organ temperament using a foot pedal.

Moreover, as a fixed-pitch instrument often found in churches, the organ has always been a focus of discussion among music scholars, theologians, and philosophers as they debate the broader implications of pure intervals. In an instrument that allows tuning changes in real-time, therefore, I found nothing less than the perfect battleground on which conflicting ideas surrounding tuning systems could be implemented. Thus I began a journey into recognizing my uncomfortable, yet fitting relationship, given my long-standing interest in aesthetic imperfection, with historical tuning systems.

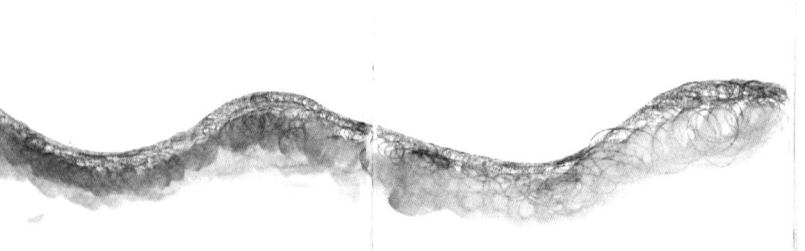

Figure 3. Excerpt from the project sketchbook by Reiko Yamada

The word "tuning" acquires new meanings when we move beyond the setup of musical instruments. In the study of soundscapes, particularly in R. Murray Schafer's seminal book *The Tuning of the World* (1977), the term "tuning" refers not only to a specific adjustment of musical pitches but also, and more generally, to one's attitude towards an overabundance of acoustic information. More specifically, whereas the verb *to tune* has traditionally meant "to adjust with respect to resonance at a particular frequency" and "to make more precise, intense, or effective,"[11] Schafer uses it instead in relation to his empirical method of soundwalking. The practice of soundwalking consists of exercises in hyper-attentive listening, in the sense of tuning *into* the world by classifying and selecting the sounds around us in a sensitive, discriminating way. When we think about constructing a tuning system, most of us imagine selecting and adding pitches in order to divide an octave. Schafer's perspective on the sound world suggests tuning as a subtractive method, beginning with the acknowledgement of the ever-lingering presence of unselected frequencies in the background.

While performances that faithfully reproduce historical repertoire necessarily require attention to specific historical temperaments, as a new music composer, I am more interested in what historical tuning systems mean to us today. Indeed, my composition *1/12 of Comma for E-Organ Solo*[12] recognizes the cacophony of the world by selecting a set

---

11 Merriam-Webster, s.v. "tune (v.)," accessed June 14, 2021 https://www.merriam-webster.com/dictionary/tune.

12 The title, "1/12 of Comma" refers to the resulting distance between pure intonation and the equal temperament in the interval of a perfect fifth.

of frequencies from historical tunings and, as these
appear and disappear, using multi-channel spa-
tialization to reveal new sets of pure perfect fifths.
Keeping pure perfect fifths in temperaments such as
just intonation always has the downside of creating
incorrect intervals elsewhere. This particular composition, being full of pure perfect fifths, therefore
reveals those unavoidable discrepancies. The constant, clustered cacophony that this produces, fad-
ing in and out, reminds the audience that an unlimit-
ed number of other frequencies are always present in
the background.

Just as the debate over temperament has historically
been about more than just musical aesthetics, this
composition is not only about musical notes. The piece
is a stand against prioritizing one system over all
others, and exhibits the messiness of the balancing
act between the practical and the ideological that
arose with the development of temperament. Much as
it may look, on the surface, as though these debates
have been resolved by settling on the twelve-note
equal temperament system, anyone who learns even
a little about temperament is struck by the fact that
a problem such as preserving the simple ratios from
natural overtones (which many would consider extremely important) has never really been resolved. 1/12
of Comma for E-Organ Solo explores the struggle to

select one compromised system over another, leaving the messy consequences of such a choice on full display to the audience. After all, the debates about temperament seem to be an effort to bring order to a muddled world. With this piece, I reject the imperative that insists on solving an unsolvable problem by imposing a single system, rather than presenting several possibilities that simply take turns.

The story of historical tuning systems is the story of our struggle to accept imperfection. The very notion of organizing sounds into tuning systems

Figure 4. Aleksey Vylegzhanin performing *1/12 of Comma for E-Organ Solo* June 6, 2018 at Orgelfrühling Steiermark
©Fabian Czernovsky

 Video 1.

was a losing battle from the beginning, as a scale formed entirely of pure intervals cannot be contained within the space of an octave. In their search for a solution, music scholars and instrument makers have tried countless variations of temperaments, modified instruments, and produced philosophical and psychoacoustical explanations only to end up abandoning all perfect natural proportions (ratios) in favor of today's equal temperament. We know that equal temperament has proven its practicality and set the stage for the development of a sophisticated musical repertoire and the ensemble performances we now enjoy. The adjustments are small enough that their effects are as subtle as those of fluctuating temperature and humidity or tuning techniques, yet discussions about temperament are frequently met with uneasiness, and disagreements on this topic quickly flare up. In that respect, responses to this subject echo responses to other life situations where we have selected the most practical from among a series of fundamentally imperfect options, and made the chosen solution so ubiquitous that our senses have become used to it and we have forgotten all other possible choices.

In my composition *524288=531441 for Violin and E-Organ*[13], I wanted to confront the uneasiness and

---

[13] The numbers 524288 and 531441 together refer to the Pythagorean comma, one of the discrepancies in pure intonation tuning.

insecurities associated with this topic. Obviously, in musical performance, we typically consider uneasiness and insecurity to be the opposite of what one expects from a good performance. Without the courage and open-mindedness of my collaborators, violinist Barbara Lüneburg and organist Aleksey Vylegzhanin, the project would not have been possible. In this work, the tuning of an organ, traditionally an instrument of fixed tuning, is made "unfixed" via the use of the DynTune pedal. The score is written in such a manner that the two instrumentalists are constantly in and out of tune with each other, making the performers genuinely insecure and forcing them to struggle with tuning on stage. For the organ part, I used Pythagorean and meantone 1/4 syntonic comma[14], combined with the traditional rules of functional harmony to create an environment where perfection and imperfection coexist.

The score excerpt (fig. 5) shows a four-voice chorale-like texture following an otherwise simple constant harmonic progression. However, a change in the tuning triggered by the tuning pedal introduces a complex recurring transformation.

---

14 Pythagorean tuning makes all the fifths perfectly consonant, and as a result, all the major thirds and major sixths are too wide. In quarter-comma meantone system, the perfect fifth is flattened by one quarter of a syntonic comma in order to obtain justly intoned major thirds.

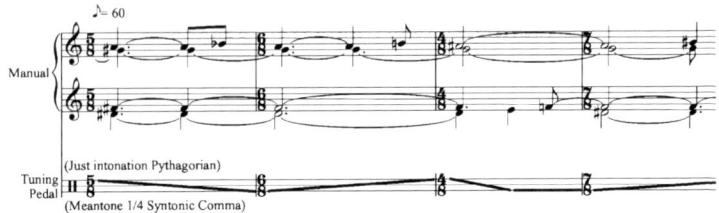

Figure 5. Excerpt of the organ part from the score *524288=531441 for Violin and E-Organ* by Reiko Yamada

While the relationship between the four organ "voices" is vertically consistent, the organist provides an irregular and subtle series of changes by adopting varying tempo and an imprecise live operation of the pedal. The result is a mixture of pre-programmed multi-part superimpositions constantly changing in relation to each other, with the organist's musical judgment (through timing changes) coming into play in real time. This process forces the other musician, a violinist, to constantly adjust her intonation in front of the audience.

Essentially, I aimed to create something similar to the effect of *sawari*, a noise maker built into certain Japanese instruments, delicately adjusted to create a flawed effect following the traditional aesthetic concept of imperfection. However, I also wanted to remain entirely within the Western music vocabulary, without copying Japanese practices. Rather than creating this effect within a single instrument, I implemented it within the relationship between two instruments on stage. The organist moves between

Figure 6. Excerpt from the project sketchbook. by Reiko Yamada.

Video 2.

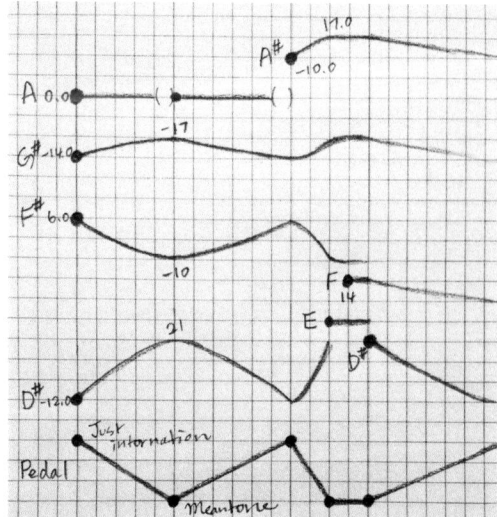

just intonation and meantone tuning (using the new MIDI tools) and the violinist tries constantly to be in tune with the organ. This is not, in other words, the expression of a Japanese alternative to Western models, but rather an exploration of Western music's own internal problems, using parallels with Japanese principles, to create new aesthetic effects.

❖   ❖   ❖

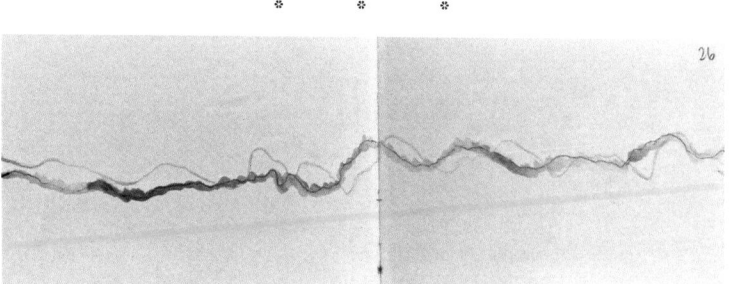

Figure 7. Excerpt from the project sketchbook by Reiko Yamada

Tempering pitched instruments and, in turn, ensembles, forces us to determine what our priorities are when we use sounds. In this world full of nuance, perhaps one way to approach this is to try deselecting the default option and continuing to explore the issue while recognizing its unsolvable nature. Deciding to upset the established order to revisit our priorities and alternatives could help us acknowledge the richness of the nuanced world, and to accept our imperfect capabilities.

I recognize that all my research and creation during my residence at a European research institute were made possible by the advancest of modern digital technologies. Only in this environment, where resources are abundant, and I was far from my homeland, was it possible for me to come to terms with the delicate and complex issues of comfort and discomfort, perfection and imperfection, and to mirror my discomfort by making a compromise with the solution of equal temperament (itself a compromise) in order to search for my own solutions to this quandary. Only then was I able to advocate for non-Western approaches to the Western historical tuning system.

Figure 8. Excerpt from the project sketchbook. by Reiko Yamada

In conclusion, I present another example of a radical solution to the issue of temperament in *7:8 for performer and fixed media*.[15] The work, full of samples from various organ sources in a variety of tunings, was put together as a fixed media work, thereby entirely avoiding the limitations intrinsic to acoustic fixed-pitch instruments as well as the problem of ensemble playing with multiple players in multiple tuning systems. Both the performer's movements and the musical motifs are inspired by the mechanics of the organ. However, the performer never "plays" the organ but instead evokes through their movements the ever-imperfect adjustments of the organ's mechanics to temperaments as compromised, imperfect solutions to an unsolvable problem. This collaborative creation strives to find as yet unnamed connections in the subtle intermedia between the sounds and movements in the organ space, and to suggest a radical role for the performer in this context. To find a way out of the unsolvable problem of temperament might require rethinking and reframing some unquestioned standards of the musical performance tradition, perhaps going as far as to reimagine the very role of the musical performer.

---

15 The simple acoustic ratio of 7:8 falls in-between major second and minor third, unable to fit in the conventional Western twelve-note tuning system.

Figure 9. Co-creator and performance artist Christina Lederhaas during the premiere of *7:8 for performer and fixed media.* June 6, 2018 at Orgelfrühling Steiermark ©Fabian Czernovsky.

 Video 3.

Acknowledgements

The author would like to thank Nicolas Trepanier, Brian Cherney, Wendy Gan, Marko Ciciliani and Barbara Lüneburg for valuable discussions and suggestions on the manuscript, as well as the Rainbow Coalition at Radcliffe and Antoine Reserbat-Plantey for the inspiration to write this text. Special thanks to the editor, Alejandra Cardenas, the proofreader, Kirstin Cameron and the team at Radical Sounds of Latin America, without whose assistance and keen insights, this article would not have been possible. The author is supported by ICFO (Institute for Photonic Sciences) and the artistic research described in this article was supported by St.A.i.R. (Styria Artist in Residence Scholarship).

References

Carlos, Wendy. 1987. "Tuning: At the Crossroads." *Computer Music Journal* 11, no. 1: 29-43. Accessed June 23, 2021. https://doi.org/10.2307/3680176.

Isacoff, Stuart. 2009. *Temperament: How music became a battleground for the great minds of Western civilization*. New York: Random House, Inc.

Schafer, R. Murray. 1977. *The Tuning of the World*. New York: A.A. Knopf.

Noise Vivarium: Spectral Radicalism

D'ANDRADE is a non-binary musician, poet, and author, whose conceptual approach to Afro-futurism and decolonial theory develops investigative works on new narratives and counter-narratives through sound design, coding, archives, and gatherings. Their current research focuses on the project Onomatopia, which is in development towards a master's degree in Art in Context at the University of Arts of Berlin, through sound, poetry, and digital games.

Introduction

A spectrogram is a visual representation of the frequency spectrum of a signal that varies with time. While there is much scientific material written about spectral studies in relation to sound, this article intends to focus on the spectral aspects of sound and how, by using digital media, we can achieve a visual and hyper-sensory experience of inaudible musicality. In this analysis, we will journey together to engage with this as existential poetics, aesthetics, and the desire for political re-existence. How can we analyze the spectrogram of a queer person? What does the representation this analysis produces mean from an integral view of sound and archive?

This article starts from the basis of three primary concepts—concepts that will help us become familiar with some of the authors and audiovisual material that guided the structure of the Noise Vivarium project. The foundations of the project were created from the study of silence and aspects of ecology, nature, and human activities, connected through a continuous flow of *a priori* understandings. The first concept is *radical listening*, a method for analyzing vocal relations and dissent through sound. The second concept is the *spectral archive,* inspired by the Manifesto Espectral of the Technodruids. The final part of the analysis involves an in-depth look at the term *techno-poetics* as established by Louis Chude-Sokei in his book *The Sound of Culture: Diaspora and Black Technopoetics*.

Radical Listening

Clarification of what is meant by radical listening involves a direct dialogue with Jacques Ranciere's book *The Ignorant Schoolmaster,* which can be read on several levels. The book primarily concerns what Ranciere discovered in the archives of Joseph Jacotot, an exiled Frenchman and teacher. In 1818, Jacotot discovered an unconventional teaching method that spread panic throughout the cultured community of Europe. Knowing no Flemish, Jacotot found himself able to teach French to Flemish students who knew no French. Jacotot concluded from this that it is possible to teach without the need for explanation, but simply by keeping learners engaged in discovery through the link of something they hold in common (Ranciere, 1991). From this postulate, Ranciere built his theory and method for intellectual emancipation - a method initiated by Jacotot, which would allow, for example, illiterate people to teach.

Ranciere considers a chain of arguments against the thesis of the equality of intelligence, which he quickly dismisses by pointing out that the progressive intellectual consensus believes, as he does, that intelligence cannot be measured (Ranciere 1991, 1-18). However, his method ignores that the sources of human classification are not exclusively about intelligence. Other determinants have been argued to be the reasons for the superiority/inferiority nexus, which will be referred to in this text, as they relate to queer and racialized bodies.

The Noise Vivarium project starts from the principle of the intellectual venture. Within this framework, a pedagogical methodology was established in which the presence of a master or even the performativity of knowledge of a school environment did not prevail. Instead, an active critique of the hierarchies of educational processes and the questioning of how to work on emancipating the participants was proposed. The whole project was developed on the basis of shared and collective knowledge; workshops served as a space for the participants to contribute to the direction of the project and the possible results.

In early 2020 in Berlin, a series of communication workshops, organized with the support of the Durchstarten program for new cultural educators, focused on young artists within the Black, Indigenous, and People of Color (BIPoC) and Queer spectrum. The workshop series took Jacques Ranciere's ideas in *The Ignorant Schoolmaster as their point of departure*. Teachers and learners were therefore placed in the same relational and political position, and moved around according to the load of knowledge they each brought with them. There was no one transmitting knowledge or performing learning. Instead, stories were shared in listening sessions offered by artists Fredrika Tsai and Leila Hussain to create a sonic map of thoughts, desires, and new ideas to build a new position of artists in collectives, teamwork, and collaborative methods.

The first meetings were based on Gayatri Spivak's text *Can the Subaltern Speak?* which analyses, through a postcolonial perspective, to whom the right to speak is reserved, and how the right to speak guarantees a certain existential quality. These encounters inspired a discussion on structural racism, as well as problematizing the migration crisis as a basis for understanding how BIPoC bodies are silenced or under-represented at various levels in geopolitical contexts. The recorded noise, both vocal and ambient, became the key material for these workshops, given that we started from the understanding that everything that can be condensed in time-space is noise, including politics. Thus, in contraposition, we characterized silence as something physically non-existent but which exists primarily as an idea to bridge Spivak's silence into a decolonial acoustic. Noisy silence, as defined in the workshops, was inspired by the approach of decoding sound and micro-social similitude as something that is in constant transformation, and is not lost spatially, as it becomes impermanent in constant circulation, the same process existing in memorization, archiving, and emotional openness.

When we speak, we emit sound, we sculpt the surrounding air using architecture and geographical accident to shape it. Through recording, the content of what is spoken, when organized into language, takes on new characteristics from a spatial perspective of acting, archiving, and unfolding what is communicated—not lost in the air, but propagated to live in the spectral dwelling. It is thus possible to record conversations, not only as a tool of documentation and archiving, but also as a poetic manifestation of a certain ephemeral moment, a landscape, or an emotion.

Radical listening takes place in the moment after the noisy silence, when the awareness of sound and politics is clear in the room. This was strongly influenced by Grada Kilomba's ideas when the author points out an imposed silence in tortured voices, and in the dimension in which she dwells when writing. In her work, Kilomba posits writing as a way of materializing the voice, of abandoning the position of being the "other" to become "self". Writing is a resource for becoming a subject and no longer an object, the exotic, the non-human, the hierarchically inferior. It entails having the power to speak your own words: "I become the absolute opposition to what the colonial project predetermined" (Kilomba, 2019, p.28). Writing becomes a political act. Writing can be an act of decolonization, specifically through the process in which we stop being objects and become subjects. The inspiration to think object to subject, according to Kilomba, is derived from the seminal author bell hooks,[1] of speaking with one's mouth, writing with one's own words. In the second chapter ("Who can speak?"), based on a 1995 dialogue with Gayatri Spivak, Kilomba stresses the question of "whether the subaltern can speak", also invoking the intellectual Patricia Hill Collins as they think about the subject and the conditions of the enunciation of speech.[2] The act of speaking is a negotiation between the one who speaks and the one who listens. Listening, in this sense, is an authorization towards the speaker. Such a process constitutes a structure of knowledge validation with hierarchical dimensions that preserve white supremacy. Given this scenario, the question is: how can a black person,

---

[1] For more about bell hooks see: hooks, bell. 1989. *Talking Back: Thinking Feminist, Talking Black*. Boston: South End Press.

[2] Collins, Patricia Hill. 2000. Black Feminist Thought. *Knowledge, Consciousness, And the Politics of Empowerment*. New York: Routledge.

racialized and with gender binarism imposed on them, produce knowledge in the academic context? Once again, the question seems to lead back to "who can speak and under what conditions?" There is no point in speaking if there is no structure that allows one to be heard.

Here we can eclipse Ranciere's intellectual emancipation critically in the context of bodies outside cis-normativity by bringing radical listening into the practical realm through the creation of spaces and experiences in which learning becomes horizontal and accepts connections with a broad political sense of diversity. The illiterate philosophers, who do not display the overly conservative characteristics of institutional canons, provoke the appearance of a new type of intellectual. This new intellectual does not belong to the ambivalent game of belonging or not belonging, but rather radicalizes listening and has their praxis in survival and re-existence—the surviving intellectual.

The field recording

The field recording of the workshops served as a tool when it came to composing with these voices, translating the whole process of radical listening into spectral tones, using digital tools, delays, and frequency shifting. All vocal elements of the discussions were transformed into emotional soundscapes. In the Noise Vivarium sound archive, there is no precise documentation of what was said in a certain situation, who said it, or how it was said, but only a noise record of the sound spectrum and whose interpretative capabilities. According to the participants, speech as a constituent of power still provides a legitimation, and *noise silence* is then a form of protest intrinsic to the system of dogmatic silencing generated by colonial institutions (schools, churches, universities, etc.). Instead, the workshops reached several critical conclusions in relation to Grada Kilomba and Spyvak's critique about the moment after subalternity, i.e., when the subaltern gains a voice, and this vocalism becomes a tool for easy manipulation and appropriation in the context of the prevailing colonial hegemony. Speaking, shouting, or vociferating is not the only step—there also exists the step of re-appropriating the sound or speech of the one who is considered subaltern. The use of abstract noise was a strong element during the workshops, in creating a soundscape composed of a range of frequencies, loops, and feedbacks, characterized by a connection with non-human cosmologies and inaudible perspectives in particular. Noise Vivarium is primarily research for a new ecology of sound, based on radical accessibility, decoloniality, and synaesthetic poetry.

Spectral Archive

The spectral archive is a term I coined to be able to analyze the sound material of Noise Vivarium. We started by mixing artistic techniques, such as field recording documentation, noise production, and spectrogram analysis with free software, to create an emotional and poetic clip of three South American queer bodies that participated in the project. The workshops with Joa Assumpção, Nicole Desposito, and Walla Capelobolo were the last of the series that concluded the first phase of the workshops, focusing on a critical reflection about borders, trans-lives, and poetics.

The term *spectral* refers to the Technodruid's *Manifesto Espectral,* made anonymously in February 2019 in the City of London, in the context of the TecnoXamanism project. The Technodruids present the manifesto in poetic form, using elements of the Amazonian indigenous cause, coloniality, and paradigms of technocratic capitalism. What is interesting about this manifesto is its evocation of the Anti-Narcissus through the ecology of sound or even the noisecracy (*Manifesto Espectral*, 2019). They elaborate the pagan polyphony of the tropics that navigates a warrior ancestry, its archive, in the end, found in orality like a wave propagation, condensed in the digital archives.

To decolonize the bowels, put your two fingers to the throat,
  to decolonize the thought,
    to hack the unconscious
     To know the other, the mirror
      let's do it in dream, let's dream in action!
        Show your face Anti-Narcissus
                             Technodruidas

The Anti-Narcissus character refers to those people without mirrors in the struggle for a counter-narrative against the technical capitalist, leading to a reflection on the spectrum and its propagative and diffusive dimensions. Spectral Radicalism exists in radio, tv, internet broadcast, in the international traffic of forbidden information. It is the tool of the exiled Anti-Narcissus, invigorating forces against the colonial catastrophe. In turn, the myth of Narcissus, of the beautiful young man who falls in love with himself and only himself, is fought in spectral radicalism through the vociferation of existences suppressed by cis-heteronormativity.

Nicole Desposito: Limits of Affection

In Sunset, Nicole Desposito's spectrogram, colors in linear scale were chosen. The sound frequencies as can be perceived in fig.1 transmit calmness, with the warm tones being enveloped by the blue blanket. Nicole's entire dialogue is permeated by these tones, connecting to the fact that there is a certain control

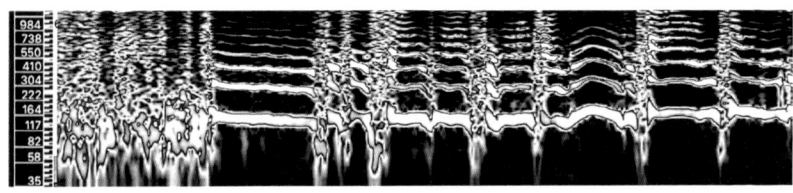

Figure 1. Sunset, the spectrogram of Nicole Desposito, Noise Vivarium, 2020.

required to deal with the subject while keeping emotions protected. Nicole's case is extremely important for this analysis because it is directly connected to trans-lives in the dynamics of relationships in the cis-hetero normative world. The gaze, or even the expectation, that passes through the cis gaze is in fact the most widely known and used sexual and affective dynamic in the social environment. When viewed through the glasses of a trans perspective, this becomes extremely painful due to the process of becoming trans and the differentiation that the individual undergoes. There is a need to find a way of coping, of dealing with withdrawals, and ideas that no longer coordinate on a larger social plane. One of the biggest problems lies in the affective issue and the particular brand of social suffering a trans person goes through due to the moral judgment they are subjected to, as well as the institutional burden of criminalization of allegedly deviant bodies. Nicole described her recent affective relationship, beginning during the Covid-19 viral pandemic in Brazil, and how its dissolution became a place of deep and experiential self-knowledge.

Nicole chose to present a poetic diary about herself, offering a self-analysis regarding the aspects of the trans body being subject to desire and the constant need to fulfil fetishistic fantasies based on cis-heteronormativity. The critical point is to realize that suffering is fully connected to a subaltern and silenced femininity; a differentiated option of desire, yet not taken to the second most serious level of relationship. The boundaries imposed on queer bodies are directly interrelated with structural racism, classism, and gender, often devaluing black and trans people, who are considered second-class partners or reduced to sexual utility. One of the ways sometimes used to overcome the trauma of rejection is to hold to a self-hypersexualization of these bodies, a complex form of self-defence and an act of survival act. This act makes conscious the exoticization and devaluation of these bodies through the same tool of objectification. For example, the body of a trans woman can meta-critically denounce patriarchal gender dogmas, as well as implicitly enable the displacement of prevailing normativity to the empowerment of that which diverges, using beauty, femininity, and care, which establish power relations based on gender binarism. Loving a trans, black body, or even a body that bears colonial traces, enables the reactivation of relational dynamics, creating a new emotion. The black or trans body, suffering the love rejection typical of the cis-heteronormative gender war, gains as a coefficient the tools for self-reflection on what love outwith gender binarism is, how these emotions are healed, and what is left in their place to overcome. Nicole's diary delves into the experience of becoming a woman in a cis-normative practical format and going through the relationship crisis as a woman in an experiential way, but with a trans positioning. Beyond the feeling of loss and loneliness, we have a self-reflective emotion and a criticism of the binary world.

Joa Assumpção: Frontiers of Language

The spectrogram (fig.2) of the artist and educator, Joa Assumpção, chose magmatic colors on a linear scale. The variations of gain, pitch, and volume are represented in the intensities of the colors. Assumpção's speech presents a constant intensity because the warm monologue is linked to experiences of dissidence that shaped her worldview. The speech was made out of fragments of the artist's coursework for her degree in pedagogy at the Universidade Federal Fluminense. The text was used in the workshop to create a performance script based on fragments, where the artist could perform these in a sequence of short audio.

Figure 2. Magnetic colors, spectrogram of Joa Assumpção. Noise Vivarium, 2020

Assumpção's audio material is directly related to language, poetry, and blackness, dialoguing with black lives as they are schooled through a white and cis-hetero-normative gaze. The artist's performative reading leads us to a reflection on auto-ethnography and how knowledge production can permeate through and to the body by putting conventional academic epistemologies into discussion for critique.

"For a black writing" is one of the collocations that point to Assumpção's thinking, in a radical positioning on knowledge production that takes on the misadventures of textual creation and the oral practice so important to black and indigenous cultures. For Abdias do Nascimento, Afrodescendants can adhere to–or choose not to adopt–an international black perspective. Although most African descendants assume forms of national identities, this does not mean that a black international perspective has not previously existed among people of African descent. One could argue that the black international perspective has had a significant impact on black people in the African

Diaspora. The Haitian revolution is an example of how populations of African ancestry were inspired by the struggles taking place. In all parts of the Americas, the Haitian revolution inspired African descendants. More than that: the Haitian revolution became the model of black liberation, based on organizing society against slavery and guaranteeing equality for all who had African ancestry. For Assumpção, the white, elitist format is counter-revolutionary and will never embrace gender dissent and structural racism issues. To understand the artist's archive, we need to understand the term "*Quilombismo*" (Nascimento, 1998), which addresses the creation of spaces of resistance and a civic culture based on the emancipation of individuals imprisoned by the dogmas of white hegemonic society. The *quilombo* would be the place in which oral culture and radical listening are primordial to accepting trans, black bodies, outside any normative standard.

Walla Capelobo: Limits of the Earth

In the archive of the artist Walla Capelobo, the sound recording captures the railroad of Congonhas, in Minas Gerais, and is related to the poem by Carlos Drummond de Andrade "The Biggest Train in the World" (Drummond, 1984). For his participation in the archive, Walla was interested in addressing the aesthetic aspects of natural

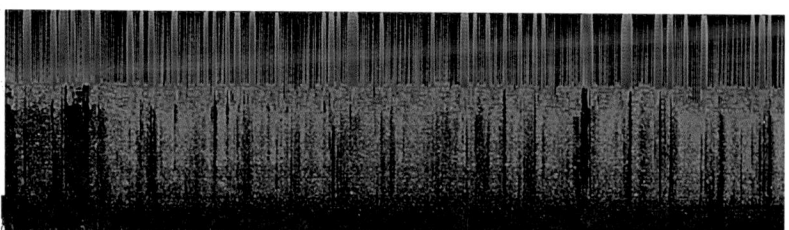

Figure 3. Fruit Salad, spectrogram of Walla Capebolo. Noise Vivarium, 2020.

resources and how colonial bodies are managed in the same way, through expropriation, exploitation, and depletion.

Mineral extractivism is one of the central axes in Walla's work, an auto-ethnographic reference to his having been raised in the Brazilian state responsible for much of the mining economy in South America. The mineral sector and its environmental risks only became known to the general Brazilian and international public after the failure of the tailings dam in Minas Gerais. Thus, the mining model is interpreted by Walla as a field of knowledge and embodiment. The artist's intervention consists of deepening the reading of the territory or space, the results reveal the importance of the poetic text as an instrument of critical and broad perception with territorial implications.

The sound of the train connects the late industrialization of the Brazilian context to the need for international acceptance as a modern country, in counterpoint to a wild nature that harbors the resources necessary for this modernization. The Brazilian drama continues in the critical paradigm of "the good savage" (Rousseau, 1996), as an anthropological analysis of the formation of Brazilian distinctions of political-social stereotypes, which intend a fixing of identity, based on a forest purism. Here we can establish an interesting counter-hegemonic narrative tool, which the Noise Vivarium project intends to fulfil at the conceptual level, in the ecology of sounds, as well as in the relationship between nature and silence, connected through the subalternity often projected on the feminine. Nature being the place of the feminine and, at the same time, presenting no language intelligible to man, it is notorious that silence is exploited in multiple ways within a colonialist, patriarchal, and expropriating mentality. The feminine here is not gender-based, but rather a set of epistemologies, rules of identification, and pedagogies, which are posited as femme. Colonial bodies are to some extent femme bodies, in terms of the domination process, directly connected to the borders of the land. "The resources of patriarchal maintenance are sustained in the exploitation or even in the creation of the feminine", leading us to the analysis of "technocratic capitalism", in Louis

Chude-Sokei's words, in which he points to the implicit relations existing between machines, raciality, and gender (Chude-Sokei 2016, 131-148.). Chude-Sokei points to the formation of capitalism based on the colonial agrarian project of the plantations and how this racialization of the black body is related to infinite free labor, similar to that of a robot, with ambiguous or even non-existent sexuality. The author takes us on a journey into Caribbean theory, making it possible to understand the strange love relationship between blacks and machines. Musical instruments are the main engine of this connection. In Capelobo's intervention, the train assumes the same role as a colonial body, crossing borders and distributing nature's resources.

Unarchiving

Noise Vivarium is an ongoing project that has no completion deadline, and is intending to become a tool for developing other works with artists interested in producing content for this archive. With all that in mind, Noise Vivarium is always unarchiving since it constitutes a direct critique of the classic institutional archives, in which queer and black bodies are often represented in racial and scientific categories. The project intends to test the possibility of archive production through refusal. This same refusal argues for the abolition of archives, which subject colonial bodies to white observation.

Drawing on Tina Campt's suggestion that refusal is not just a strategy of resistance, but a fundamental negation of the terms through which oppression is exercised upon black life (Campt 2017), Noise Vivarium further asks what kinds of engagements with colonial archives are available if we wish to refuse the archive's violent structuration of the present. Noise Vivarium's spectral archive is an addendum to the unarchiving movement, strongly connected with the computing term in which you must decompress a file to access it, an increasingly normalized cultural practice in contemporary society. Digital archives then gain a disruptive capacity when it comes to the production and organization of archives. With the aesthetics of informational data as the great surface on which these archives rest, we advance a different feeling than that which extensive collections used to have, based on secrecy, mysticism, and a sacralization of knowledge locked away in departments. Unarchiving offers the file for decoding, and from the file, it can unfold into more files, always decompressing. In Noise Vivarium, sound is stored directly in digital form, and as images and codes that can be revisited and decoded through an artistic lens and engaged with mainly through inter-relational practices. Sound as not only something audible, but as a tool for socialization.

References

Candido, A. 1984. "A vida ao rés-do-chão". *Para gostar de ler*. Andrade, Carlos Drummond et al. São Paulo: Ática.

Fortes, L. R. S. 1996. *Rousseau: o bom selvagem*. São Paulo: FTD.

Kilomba, Grada. 2019, *Memórias da plantação: episódios de racismo cotidiano*. Translated by Jess Oliveira. Rio de Janeiro: Editora Cobogó.

Chude-Sokei, Louis Onuorah. 2016. *The Sound of Culture: Diaspora and Black Technopoetics*. Middletown: Wesleyan University Press.

Nascimento, Abdias do. 2019. *O Quilombismo*. São Paulo: Editora Perspectiva.

Rancière, Jacques. 1991. *The ignorant schoolmaster: five lessons in intellectual emancipation*. Stanford, California: Stanford University Press.

Spivak, Gayatrik Chakravarty. (1995). "Can the Subaltern Speak?". In *The post-colonial studies reader*. Edited by Bill Ashcroft, Gareth Griffiths, and Helen Tiffin. London: Routledge, p. 24-28.

Campt, Tina M. 2017. *Listening to Images*. Duke University Press Books

Technodruidas. 2019. "Manifesto Espectral" *Tecnoxamanismo*. Last modified 20 June, 2021. https://tecnoxamanismo.wordpress.com/2019/02/18/manifesto-spectral/